DESIGNING FOR COMPACT SPACES

SQUEEZING IT IN

RIBA ✺ Publishing

MARY LESLIE

© RIBA Publishing, 2022

Published by RIBA Publishing, 66 Portland Place, London, W1B 1AD

ISBN 9781859469132

The right of Mary Leslie to be identified as the Author of this Work has been asserted in accordance with the Copyright, Designs and Patents Act 1988 sections 77 and 78.

British Library Cataloguing-in-Publication Data
A catalogue record for this book is available from the British Library.

Commissioning Editor: Elizabeth Webster
Assistant Editor: Clare Holloway
Production: Jane Rogers
Designed and typeset by Mercer Design, London
Printed and bound by L.E.G.O S.p.A Italy
Cover image: Amy (AJ) Adams

While every effort has been made to check the accuracy and quality of the information given in this publication, neither the Author nor the Publisher accept any responsibility for the subsequent use of this information, for any errors or omissions that it may contain, or for any misunderstandings arising from it.

www.ribapublishing.com

CONTENTS

ACKNOWLEDGEMENTS

When Susannah Lear, acting commissioning editor at RIBA Publishing, first approached me about this book in 2018 I little realised what it would involve. The RIBA team, particularly Elizabeth Webster, Clare Holloway and Richard Blackburn, were infinitely patient in steering me through the process. I would also thank my research assistants, Kate Anderson and Annie Reddaway, the former on the technical side and the latter on the administration.

Space precludes me from mentioning all the amazing interior designers, architects and photographers who helped me write this book. You know who you are, however, a particular thank you goes to Dean Keyworth, Philippa Thorp, Matthew Wood, Darren Oldfield, Mary Arnold-Forster and Benjamin Tindall who inspired me as I disappeared down the rabbit hole of online research. Eva Byrne, Pauline Lorenzi-Boisrand, Bertrand Fompeyrine and Kumiko Ishiguro amongst others were wonderfully obliging as I widened my search to Europe and Japan.

A special mention goes to Nina Campbell who taught me so much about bespoke design and decoration which runs through every aspect of this book.

Finally, my infinitely patient husband, Geoffrey, who supported me in so many ways, and would probably hope I am never tempted to write another one.

ABOUT THE AUTHOR AND ILLUSTRATOR

Mary Leslie is an interior designer with over 40 years of experience working primarily on residential projects in the UK and overseas. She founded her own practice in 1996 after many years running the Interior Design Department for internationally-renowned designer Nina Campbell. She is a former Vice Chairman of the BIDA (now BIID) and a former Chairman of the BIDA Charitable Foundation.

Cover design and illustrations by Amy (AJ) Adams. AJ is an artist, illustrator and author whose work is all about architecture. She lives and works in London and is a graduate of Camberwell College of Arts and the London College of Fashion.

FOREWORD

In the words of Elsie de Wolfe, suitability, practicality and proportion are the cornerstones of good design, and this is all the more important when space is restricted. Nothing is more irritating than a beautiful house that simply doesn't work and isn't fit for purpose.

Space, certainly in cities, is expensive, and all the square footage needs to earn its keep. It's crucial to have a place for all the necessities of a home in a way that makes living seamless and easy. Storage is vital, as a small space must be kept tidier than one where there is the luxury of extra closets. In the future it is likely that our homes will also be our offices, certainly for a few days a week, so this must be included too. Added to all of the above is the need for the interiors to be attractive, exciting and comfortable, as well as being what the client wants! When you have the luxury of space all this becomes easier, but properties are getting smaller and having to work harder than ever.

Like all good ideas, when you see one you wonder why it hasn't been done before: *SQUEEZING IT IN* is packed with inspiring and well-conceived answers to these dilemmas, and will be immensely useful to the professional designer as well as the amateur. It is rich with plans, sketches and elevations to explain fully the process to the reader, as well as photographs of the final result.

The elephant in the room is usually the budget, and this is so important to address and understand from the beginning, and to stick to. The notion, discussed in this book, that thinking time should be factored into the design time is so wise; after all, it will eliminate many expensive mistakes later in the project. Gimmicks are not an option in a compact space. Lighting, which can make or break a design, is covered, as are laundry and kitchen needs, and all the mechanics of a home. All in all, this book will be invaluable as a checklist for anyone approaching a design project.

I commend this useful book to design students, clients, and professionals alike; bravo Mary Leslie for tackling this subject so concisely.

NINA CAMPBELL

Design is not just what it looks and feels like.

Design is how it works.

STEVE JOBS

INTRODUCTION

One of the best things about being an interior designer is that you never know what your next clients will ask of you. In your working day you might be designing a six-bedroom luxury villa by the sea for an international business executive, followed by trying to accommodate a busy family in a small cottage in Chelsea. Standing in the mud looking at a problem while your builder is excavating a basement could be followed by choosing colour schemes for a time-poor client who lives 5,000 miles away. The budgets will range from generous (which you will need when designing bespoke joinery and complicated engineering), to extremely tight for turnkey rental properties or those for first-time buyers. Whatever the client's brief or budget, it is important that you treat each commission with the same attention to detail and sympathetic outlook. This will help manage the client's expectations and ensure that you do the very best for their project.

Nowadays, space is a luxury. Most of us want enough space to spread ourselves and our possessions around comfortably, to entertain bountifully, to work constructively and sleep peacefully. For many, that luxury will not exist and when we as designers are asked to consider compact spaces, we have to use all our skills to create something new which is clever, aesthetically pleasing and practical, or to improve what is there for the benefit of our clients.

FIGURE 0.1: Mary Arnold-Forster Architects. Isle of Skye, Scotland, 2008. It is important to be proactive, creatively and practically. Including an outside shower for a holiday home helps prevent everyone from treading sand into the house.

My aim in writing this book has been to guide the designer through the possibilities and the pitfalls when squeezing life into compact spaces. It is important to remember that one person's compact space is another's decently sized room. As designers we are asked to consider both. I feel that for modern living it is useful to drop the traditional names for rooms, and instead consider what their function will be. Hence each chapter examines a function of the home, and how the designer can exploit it to improve the whole. Having different spaces in which to relax, work, cook, eat, bathe, sleep and store everything can be tricky, and doing so in a way which is creative, effective and practical while echoing the style requested by the client will always be a challenge.

There are differences between designing a spacious home and fitting multifarious functions into a smaller one. Subtle alterations can make all the difference, and a clever designer will learn how to recognise the potential of an existing property or ensure that a new build has a layout which will look wonderful but still be practical.

Every designer has to make the most of their own talents and learn when to seek advice elsewhere. The maxim 'you can do anything, but not everything' rings true in interior design. It might be tempting to save money by doing a full set of working drawings and specifying all the furnishings, fittings and equipment yourself, but is that the best use of time?

Building regulations, planning consents, licences to alter leasehold properties, structural alterations, and mechanical and electrical installations are all specialisms of their own, and these days it would be a brave interior designer who thought they could do it all themselves. A designer who works in a multidisciplinary practice will be able to

FIGURE 0.2: John Lees. 2020. At the start of a project, fitting everything into the space can seem an impossible task. Finding that every space works, while ensuring that there is empty space as well, is a very satisfying achievement.

FIGURES 0.3A AND 0.3B: Interior design by Harriet Hughes. London, 2020. What to do with a niche too small for a piece of furniture? Turn it into a drinks cabinet.

call on others on the team, but many interior designers are either sole practitioners or part of microbusinesses and need to build relationships with other experts who can be brought on to the team when necessary. For example, technology moves so fast it is often wiser to commission a lighting designer or audiovisual consultant than try to fulfil either function on your own.

The first task I always arrange for a new client is a full measured survey of the property. Tempting though it may be to gloss over details when first looking at a place with the client, while cheerfully saying 'we can knock this through' or 'let's fit the piano into this alcove', reality is often different. Moving the wall might not be feasible, and the piano might be 150mm too wide.

A client with a large budget may be able to afford radical alterations, but there will be times when the cost is prohibitive, or the solution too complicated. The survey of a building will reveal any problems such as soil stacks, chimney flues and structural walls which could prevent that bright idea from becoming a reality. Furthermore, looking at a property in plan will often reveal possibilities that might not have been apparent at the start. Bear in mind, though, that not every client can read a plan, and those glossed-over details may be useful when you explain your ideas at the next stage.

When embarking on a project we must tactfully manage client expectations of the work involved, as well as the time and cost of specifying, managing and executing the project. The client needs to understand that a small project will not necessarily cost less per square foot than a large one. It is easy at the beginning of a project to use average per square foot or square metre prices; however, you must consider the density of the small property versus a large one. The larger property will have more empty air, whereas the smaller one will be constricted, and the solutions may be more complex than the client will at first appreciate.

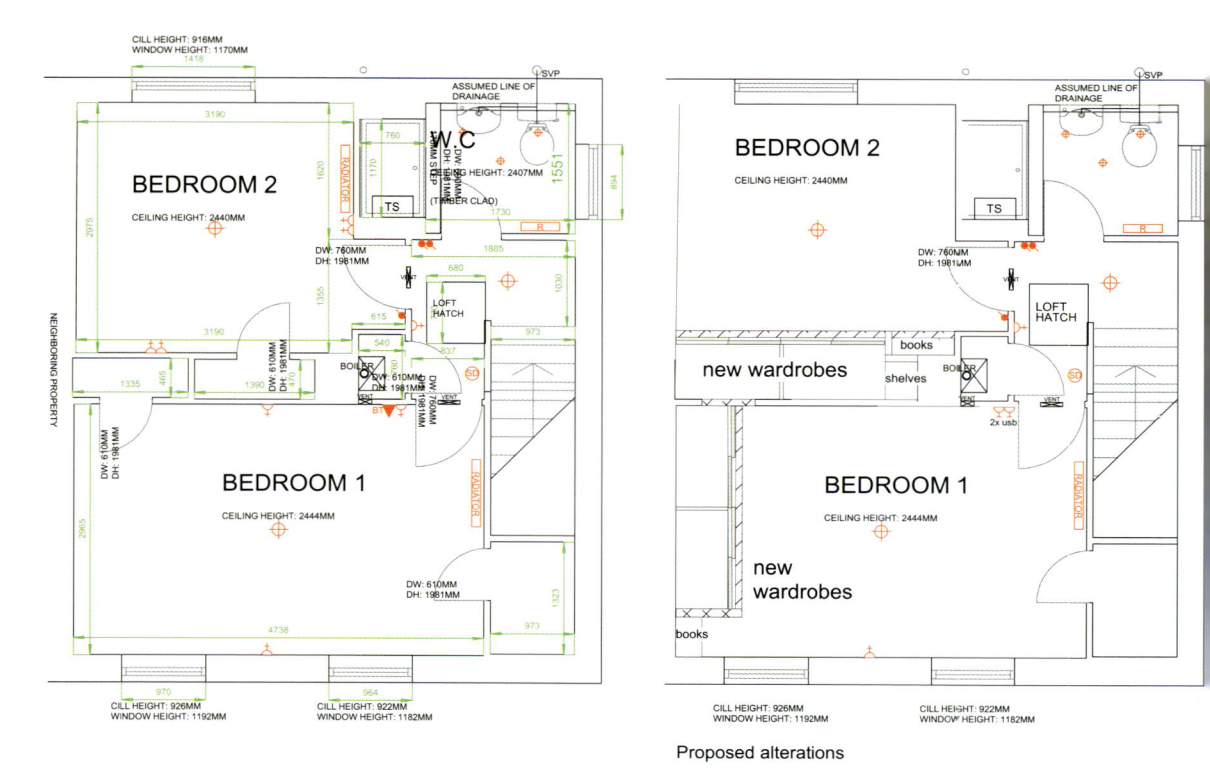

Figure 0.4: Interior design by Mary Leslie. Forfar, Angus, 2018. However small the project, a measured survey will show possibilities for the manipulation of space which may not be apparent when first on site.

FIGURE 0.5: Architecture by Mary-Arnold Forster Architects. Isle of Skye, Scotland, 2008. Always build thinking time into your fee. Gazing out at the view and gathering your thoughts will be time well spent.

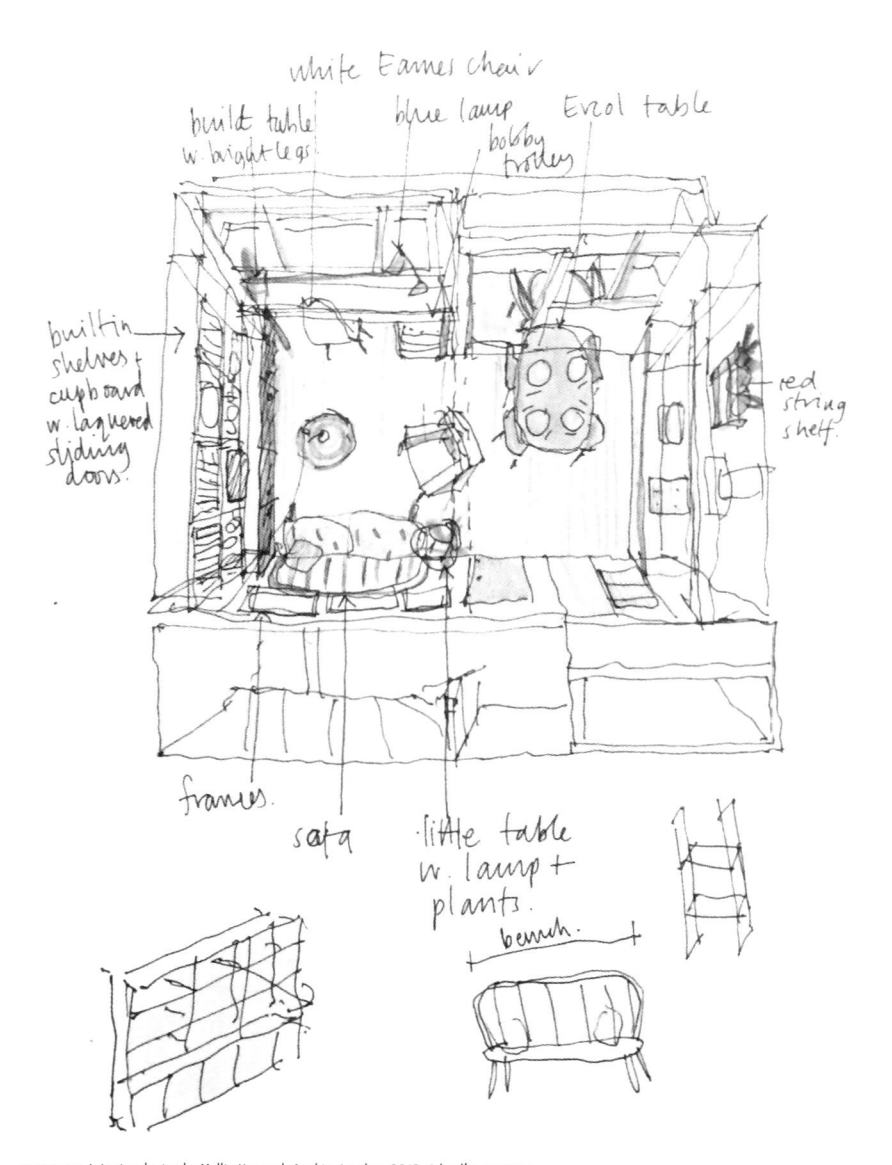

white Eames chair

built table
w bright legs!

blue lamp   Ercol table
bobby
trolley

builtin
shelves +
cupboard
w. laquered
sliding
doors.

red
string
shelf.

frames.

sofa

little table
w. lamp +
plants.

bench.

FIGURE 0.6: Interior design by Mellis Haward, Archio. London, 2010. A bird's-eye view shows how sitting, cooking, eating and working will all fit into one compact space.

There is a moment at the start of a project when you might think 'how am I ever going to fit all this in?' Many a time the designer will wish each room were six inches larger in every direction, but we must make the most of what we have. I love the moment at the beginning of the creative phase when I can think how best to manipulate the space to reach the desired outcome. If you can think in three dimensions and sketch what you are trying to achieve, even for the smallest detail, you will more likely carry the client with you.

I am a great believer in the value of a checklist, and I have offered these throughout as a trigger for the designer's creative ability. They are not definitive, but they open the mind. When you are starting the project, and presenting a solution, it is worth asking yourself:

- Does it work for the client?
- Does it enhance the space?
- Is it aesthetically pleasing?
- Is it practical?
- Does it fulfil the brief?
- Is it affordable?
- Is it allowed?

FIGURE 0.7: Architecture by Darren Oldfield Architects, interior design by Beth Dadswell of Imperfect Interiors. London, 2019. Simple architectural detailing and a careful choice of furniture and accessories bely the amount of work involved in creating this elegant pied-à-terre living area.

1

....

THE LIVING SPACE

....

Of all the areas in a compact home which have to be versatile, the living space is surely the one which needs to be most adaptable. Single-person households may have the luxury of spreading themselves around even the smallest of rooms as they wish; however, a family or group of people living in the same property will require very different things from their living spaces. The designer should manipulate the available area to provide as many alternatives as possible. A room might appear spacious when viewed on plan, but once all the needs of the household are taken into consideration it will soon fill up. It will help the designer if even small spaces are thought of in terms of zones, and careful consideration is put into multipurpose areas, furniture and lighting to alleviate the challenge.

The strain put on living spaces during the 2020 coronavirus pandemic shows that they will have to be considerably more flexible than previously, and the approach to their design will depend largely on whether the space is part of a period or contemporary property, or a planned new build.

FIGURES 1.1A AND 1.1B: Interior design by Harriet Forde. London, 2016. Removing the partition wall in a London terraced house allows for a better flow, particularly when combined with a full-width kitchen extension leading into the garden.

Designers will be familiar with the rows of nineteenth- and early twentieth-century houses which line the towns of Britain. Even the most modest of these generally provided a front and back parlour, with clear social distinctions. Over the past 50 years there has been a trend to knock down the wall between the two to create one larger living room. That principle works well for many, and allows a freer flow of space, light and air. When these houses were built the most important room looked on to the street; however, nowadays the preference is to have direct access from the living room to the back garden if possible. The change to less formal entertaining means that a larger through living room allows for better circulation, and a dining table at the back of the room is useful for homework, or a play area, with comfortable seating and the TV grouped around the original fireplace at the front. However, that scenario does not necessarily work if several house sharers find themselves all working from home with similar hours, not enough space in the bedrooms for everyone to have their own desks and a need for privacy around the workspace.

Many new build homes have open-plan sitting/dining/cooking spaces, which are economical to build, popular with families and easily maintained. However, the same problems will arise when people have to make so much more of their living space, and clever designs, particularly at the lower end of the market, tend to be small. Just as with the Victorian artisan's terraced house, putting up solid partitions will show precisely how compact they are.

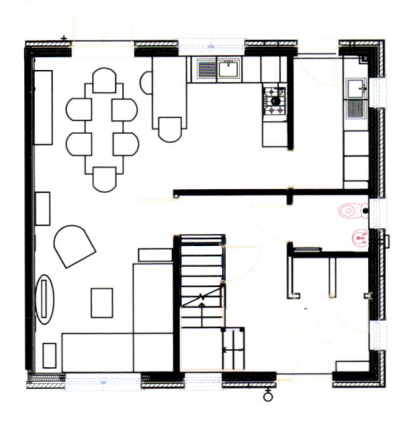

FIGURES 1.2A, 1.2B AND 1.2C: Interior design by Mary Leslie. Sutherland, Scotland, 2015. A small, new build, open-plan living room gives plenty of space for everyday living.

The greatest luxury is to have a new build home where account can be taken of all the needs of the family. It should be more of a broken-plan than an open-plan space, with enough different zones to enable everyone to have their privacy when needed. The new build does not have to be a standalone house – it might be a new use for an old warehouse, a loft or even empty office space. The latter currently have a poor reputation because of designs which may run close to contravening the regulations. However, a clever, sympathetic refurbishment can revive a redundant building and improve housing stock without using greenfield sites. Changing retail habits mean that more shops have to find new uses, and these can include clever residential and live/work spaces. Architects and designers in rural areas also have the opportunity to reuse agricultural buildings or add sympathetic new extensions to old cottages.

A new building, extension or reuse gives the opportunity to look at opening up vertically as well as horizontally, and a clever designer or architect can create a much more interesting and adaptable space by thinking holistically about opening up the whole rather than simply adding or removing walls on one level.

In a flat there is less room for change, and a compact apartment with one living room and a couple of bedrooms may require considerable rearrangement to find ways of making the space work for the best. If a house or flat has a small, separate dining room, that too will have to multitask. As people's lives change, having the extra room may prove useful, rather than the modern default of knocking the living spaces into one large area.

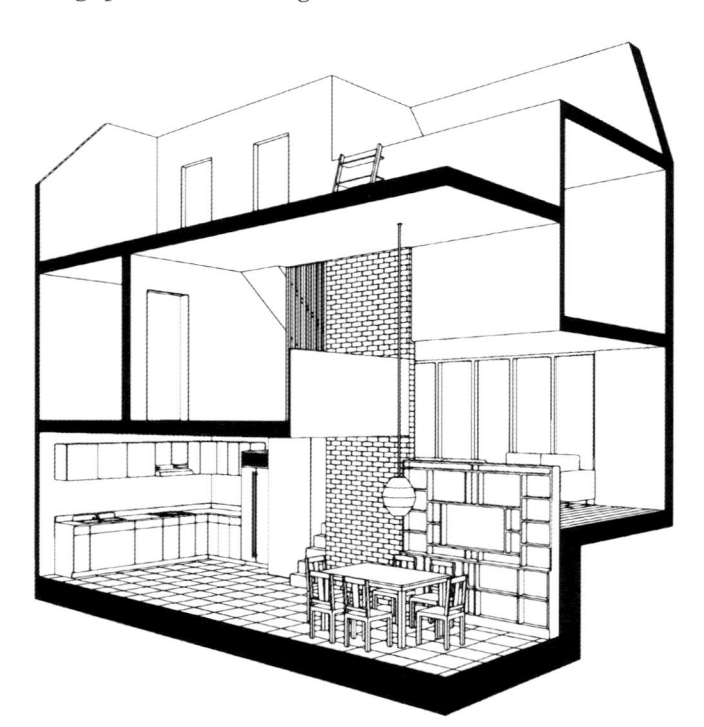

FIGURES 1.3A, 1.3B AND 1.3C: Design by Matthew Wood Architects. Upper Norwood, London, 2012. This new build mews house uses split levels to create broken spaces, allowing for interaction and privacy in equal measure.

The designer faced with a compact living space needs first to establish what it is going to be used for. As mentioned previously, it will almost certainly be needed for several different functions such as eating, sitting, entertaining, reading, craftwork, watching television, playing, working and school homework.

These considerations should be explored with the client at the briefing stage, and include the following.

- What functions can be moved elsewhere? In Chapter 4 we examine the workspace, and ideally that can be shifted into an outhouse, bedroom, landing or other corner which can be shut off at the end of the day. However, if several people are working from home day in, day out at least one will likely find themselves in the living room. If the home has a separate kitchen, does it have room for a dining table, and could this be extended to provide extra space for eating, working or playing?

- How often does the client entertain, and how many need to sit in the living room or dining area? Clearly a small sitting room will be a squeeze for eight adults, but there are ways of fitting in the occasional extra person.

- Does the client need room for hobbies such as making music, reading, embroidery or jigsaws? It is important to enquire about and listen to their particular requirements. Where are you going to put the spinning wheel, three electric guitars or model planes?

- How much time does the client spend watching television or listening to music or the radio, and what screen size would they like? Do they have a standalone hi-fi system? Do they want to be able to stream sound from room to room? In a small space the screen does not have to be vast and will probably be the easiest thing to fit in – but hopefully not over a fireplace, which usually leaves the screen too high and uncomfortable to watch. It may only be in conversation that the designer will discover the client has a set of oversized hi-fi speakers from a previous era, which absolutely have to be sited in the only spot available for a sideboard.

- How much storage is needed, if the client has a particular collection to display, or hundreds of books to accommodate? Can space be made for them in the hall or on a landing or staircase?

- If children live in the home, does the client want them to play in the living room under a watchful eye or have their toys in their own rooms, which make a much better place for all their clutter?

FIGURE 1.4: Interior design by René Dekker, London, 2015. A small TV room can become a glamorous home cinema with the right equipment and furnishings.

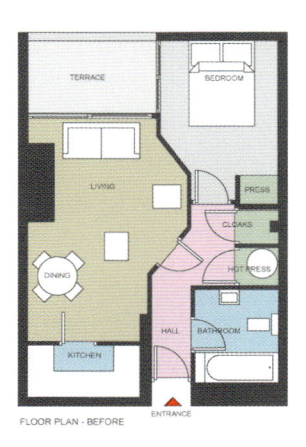
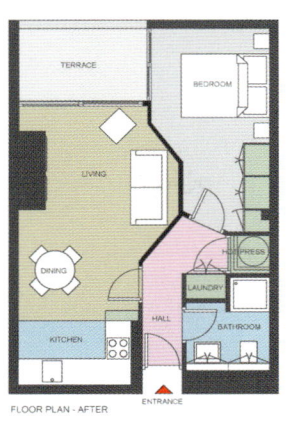

FLOOR PLAN - BEFORE   ENTRANCE

FLOOR PLAN - AFTER   ENTRANCE

FIGURE 1.5: Interior design by Eva Byrne. Dublin, 2019. Moving a door and rearranging the furniture improves the space in this small Dublin living room.

The designer's solutions will as always be driven by the client's expectations, the budget, the footprint, the use and the style.

The wise designer will start with the footprint for the whole property to see whether the existing layout is best for flow, use of space and light, and access to services. Sometimes it only takes a small adjustment to free up space which can be used better than the existing floor plan. For example, it might be possible to move or reduce the number of doorways, which creates extra wall space. It might also be possible to remove partition walls, as in the front and back rooms of a traditional, period terraced house, which gives a larger, brighter room.

Bespoke joinery can be used to create storage and multipurpose spaces. If a client is keen on books the designer might be able to add a window seat with bookcases either side, which creates both a book nook and a library. The radiator might fit under the window seat (with vents behind the seat cushion), or alternatively the space might become a toy box or filing cabinet.

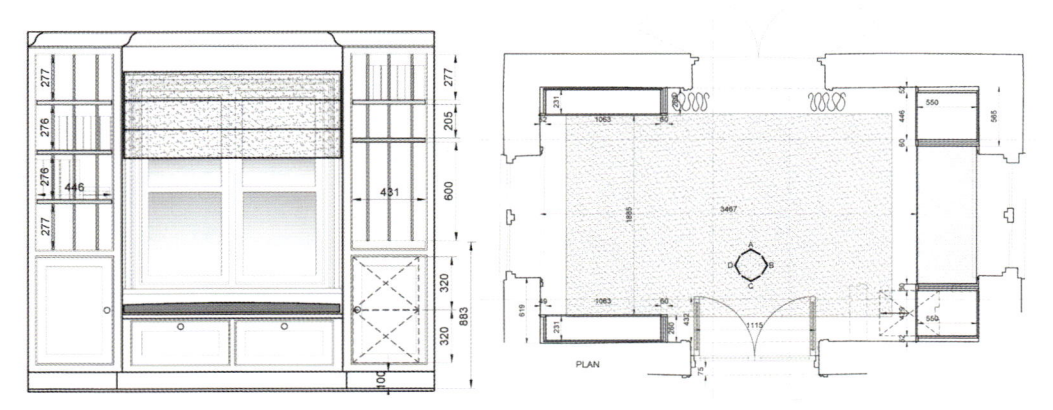

FIGURES 1.6A AND 1.6B BELOW: Interior design by Mary Leslie. Coggeshall, Essex, 2018. Accurate drawings show how a window seat and bookcases make a comfortable reading nook in this cottage sitting room.

There are so many possible places to put shelves, depending on what is to go on them. Either side of a chimney breast is the most obvious, but consider wrapping them either side of a sofa, around a door or as a room divider. The dimensions are relatively formulaic, and it is worth finding a size chart which can be referred to repeatedly. Versatility will be vital to the exercise, and the easiest way to achieve that is with adjustable shelves.

However, when designing any storage unit, it is important to consider that some fixed uprights and shelves are essential for structural integrity. That particularly applies to bookshelves, bearing in mind how heavy books and magazines are. When working out the layout, the designer will be aware that the shelf depth and the unit depth are usually different, particularly where a void is to be left at the rear of the unit for power or audiovisual cables. If cables are being dropped down inside a cupboard, the informed designer will know to specify cut-outs in the internal shelves so that the cables can drop down behind them, and also circular cut-outs in the side partitions which enable the client to pull cables through from one section to another.

For clients who cannot afford bespoke joinery there are plenty of solutions available from furniture stores. There you will find self-assembly or modular pieces to accommodate most things, from vinyl records and DVDs to books, games and ornaments.

Once the designer has decided on the footprint of the living space, they will need to consider the lighting, using all four options: natural, ambient, task and accent. Addressing these in turn helps plan the lighting for each area, bearing in mind how the client will use the space, what mood they want to create, and the practical considerations involved. Even in a compact space if the lighting requirement is complex, or there are voids, changes in level and open-plan vistas to take into

FIGURE 1.7: Interior design by Mary Leslie. Perthshire, Scotland, 2014. A simple bookcase is designed to take the weight of heavy hardbacks and make space for a basic flatscreen/soundbar combination in a small country house sitting room.

FIGURE 1.8: Interior design by René Dekker. London, 2016. Layering light is essential. Here it is used to add glamour and sparkle to a living room.

account, it is worth commissioning a lighting designer to develop the scheme. The complexities of modern lighting mean that working with a professional lighting expert will be a useful part of the learning curve for any designer.

Whether the designer develops the lighting alone or with an expert, they will need a clear furniture layout as a starting point. From there they can consider the effect of natural light and how that can be exploited within the space. Ambient, task and accent lighting should all then be layered to create different moods and atmospheres depending on the time of day and the number of potential uses for the rooms.

When considering the furniture and furnishings, designers should not be afraid of colour, even in a small space. Although many contemporary homes benefit from being painted white throughout, splashes of colour can add impact to a restricted space, with a combination of colour and texture created by the right balance of flooring, walls, window treatments and furniture. A small room intended for watching television or for use as a library could be cosy and cocooning, while a contemporary multipurpose living room may need large runs of furniture which will create a visually greater space than the reality. Designers should avoid too many

FIGURE 1.10: Interior design by Mary Leslie. London, 2004. Floaty chiffon top curtains and reflective-backed sheers protect the eye from the glare of sun on the Thames.

small pieces, which create clutter rather than layers. Banquette seats, coffee tables which become dining tables, sideboards and credenzas used as room dividers, sectional seating which fill long walls as well as corners can all create a sense of more space than might be the reality.

Large artworks can be effective in small spaces. Like colour, the designer should not hesitate to use interesting art and sculpture to add character to a room.

Window treatments can be used to trick the eye. Roman blinds which hang from the underside of the ceiling rather than a few centimetres above the window reveal create a sense of height. Heavy, full-length curtains can make a space look either grand or cosy at will, and cut out draughts at the same time. If the room has wonderful views, it may be that all the space needs is a set of sheer curtains or blinds to remove glare. If a property overlooks water, even on a higher floor, it is important to consider what happens when the sun hits the water – the reflection can be blindingly bright.

Checklist – have you asked the client:

- Who will be using the living areas of the house, and for what?

- How often does the client entertain, and in what style?

- Could any of the intended uses, such as study or work, be moved elsewhere?

- What collections, such as books or ornaments, need to be displayed in the living space? Could any of them be displayed elsewhere?

- Does the client want a large TV screen, and what other audiovisual requirements do they have? Will everything be streamed, or will the client require an AV stack? Are there large numbers of CDs or DVDs or a record collection to accommodate?

- Does the space need to have a play area for small children?

- What type of seating does the client prefer?

- How will orientation and natural light affect the space?

- Does the client already have works of art to hang in the space? Can any of them be used as a hook for the colour scheme?

- Will the budget allow for bespoke furnishings and storage, or does the designer need to incorporate self-assembly, modular or vintage items?

FIGURE 1.11: Interior design by #the_girl_with_the_green_sofa and Mairi Helena. Yorkshire, 2017. An eclectic space with an oversized sofa will lure all the family to relax and need not look out of place in a compact sitting room.

CASE STUDY 1.1 ARCHIO

FIGURE 1.12: Adding an extension, however small, can make all the difference to an old cottage.

DESIGNERS   Kyle Buchanan of Archio, and the clients

CLIENTS   A retired professional couple

BRIEF   The existing Grade II listed cottage on four floors provided three bedrooms which slept eight at a squeeze, but it had a very small living room and little room to eat. The brief was to create a new living space in place of the existing, rarely used decking, which would seat eight and free up the old living room to provide a comfortable dining room.

The clients were emphatic that the pitched roof line should not impede the view of the harbour for houses further up the hill. As an accomplished joiner and carpenter, he wanted a design that he could largely build himself, leaving only the groundworks up to the footings, the stone walls, insulation and zinc roofing materials to be done by others.

The architect and structural engineer were commissioned to deal with the planning application and listed building consent, as well as to specify the technical details and calculations to ensure the correct lines of sight, loadings and angles to create as much internal space as possible within a confined envelope.

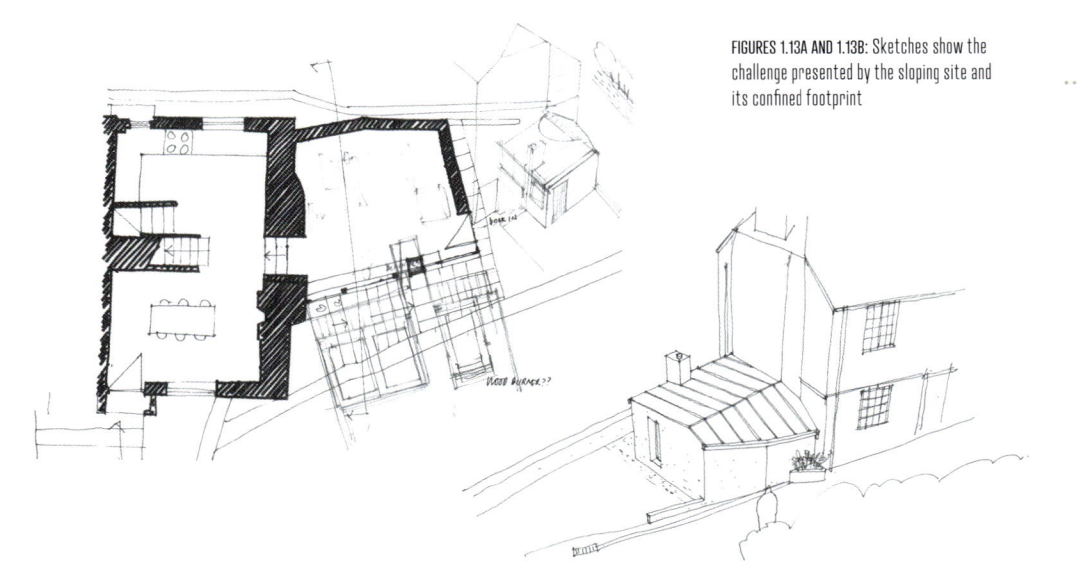

With a site in Cornwall, an architect in London and the clients moving between Cornwall and the Home Counties there were few face-to-face meetings. Fortunately, as they had known one another for a long time they were comfortable with a virtual relationship for much of the time

LOCATION   A village on the Roseland Peninsula in Cornwall

CHALLENGE   The greatest challenge in the project was the geometry. Setting out the space with its dog-leg shape, cranked roof and lowered floor was a test for all concerned, and the whole team were involved in finding a workable solution which used the angles to provide as much space as possible.

The property is a Grade II listed building within a conservation area. The planners were sympathetic to the idea of a new extension, and felt that it was a better addition to the property than the existing decking. That might have meant knocking a hole through a 200-year-old wall; however, luckily the end wall of the house had been rebuilt some 40 years ago, negating the need for anything so drastic.

In order to comply with the clients' determination to not impede the view from behind, it was necessary to set the floor a metre below ground level. Even with the lowered floor, the roof line was fairly low, so to create as much height and volume as possible the team designed a cranked roof frame which removed the need for traditional supports along the rafters.

The structural engineer found it difficult to source calculations for the beams, all of which were different, so the team, led by the client, made a sample birch ply beam and physically loaded it to ensure that the deflections met the necessary criteria.

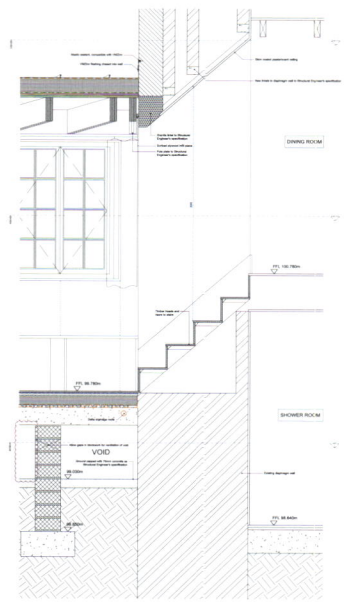

FIGURE 1.14: Steps through the new end wall connect the two living spaces, and the painted stone wall breaks up the birch ply surfaces used elsewhere.

FIGURE 1.15: The technical implications of lowering the floor are clearly demonstrated by the working drawings.

FIGURE 1.16: The cranked roof with its individual birch ply beams makes an unusual and unique ceiling for the living room.

It was important that as much timber as possible was used to allow the client to exploit his own skills, and the solution was to build an oriented strand board (OSB) shed with a birch ply panelled interior and stone cladding. The beams were constructed from three 18mm sleets of ply sandwiched together, with the remainder in 18mm or 13mm birch ply panels according to need. Timber-framed windows, also built by the client, completed the joinery works.

The limited amount of electrical work required was also carried out by the client, with the installation being fully tested and inspected for the completion certificate. The lighting is designed to highlight the curves and shadows of the beams in the unique timber ceiling. The area has a relatively mild climate for the UK, and heating could be provided by an electric heater in one corner and a wood-burning stove, whose flue runs out of its back and up though the replaced end wall.

Furniture and furnishings were kept to a minimum and designed to be low maintenance, durable and provide seating for at least eight in comfort. The window seat also provides much-needed storage, and the decorative coiled birch light fittings tie in with the overall timber theme of the decorations.

OUTCOME   The clients are delighted with the result.

After about a year of planning, calculating and building they have a design which they love, and which gives them the extra room they need. The whole space has a beautiful simplicity to it which belies the complicated calculations and setting out in the workshop needed to achieve the brief.

They particularly love the nautical references of the roof, which are so appropriate for that particular corner of Cornwall.

FIGURE 1.17: Every plane and angle from ceiling to window seat had to be individually calculated to ensure an exact fit.

CASE STUDY 1.2: SPENCER & WEDEKIND

DESIGNERS	Spencer & Wedekind
CLIENTS	An Anglo-French professional couple
BRIEF	The brief was to remodel the interior of a run-down, terraced cottage, including provision of an open-plan sitting room and kitchen/dining room leading out into the garden. The clients wanted a sophisticated interior with quirky details which would suit their lifestyle, using affordable, reclaimed materials where possible.
LOCATION	West London
CHALLENGE	The cottage was only 950 square metres in size when the clients found it. It was in a bad enough state of repair that it was on the verge of being condemned, so the first challenge was to secure the foundations, which had structural cracks, but fortunately no woodworm, rot or rising damp. (That would have involved removal of the original wooden floorboards, popping of all skirtings and architraves, and excavation and underpinning of the foundations.)

The clients also needed to extend the ground floor to make space for a new kitchen as part of the open-plan, split-level ground floor. Fortunately, as the house had only two floors and no attic conversion, they were not required to enclose the staircase in order to comply with fire regulations, allowing the designers to open up the ground floor space as much as possible.

FIGURE 1.18: This minute, terraced cottage was transformed by opening up the split level ground floor and adding a kitchen extension in the side return.

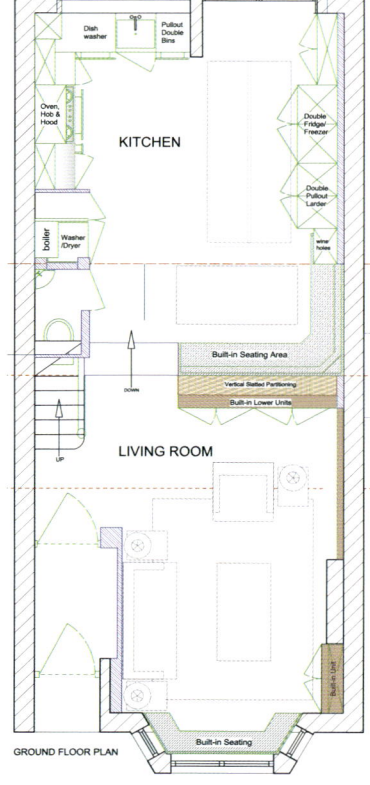

FIGURE 1.19: Renovation is a messy business. Clients need to understand what they are undertaking, including a realistic timeframe, before embarking on a major refurbishment project.

FIGURE 1.20: By building out into the side return and exploiting the change in levels between sitting, eating and cooking areas Spencer & Wedekind successfully manipulated the space to make a small cottage ground floor feel much larger.

By using the side return the designers extended the kitchen, and a glazed roof light provided much-needed light and a sense of extra space for the ground floor.

The original joinery work and floorboards were in too bad a state of repair to reuse, so the designers took the opportunity to start afresh, including replacing the skirtings, architraves and cornices. They found a source of reclaimed French oak which was cut down to a slim vol de flèche parquet design with plain planks around the fireplace, giving character to the sitting area. An unlacquered brass metal inlay was used to differentiate the two surfaces. The same design was used for the lower level running into the kitchen extension, with the inlay running along the length of the vol de flèche at random intervals.

The designers wanted to create a break between the sitting and dining areas without the original partition wall. They created a barrier to exploit the drop in levels by adding cupboards in the sitting room, which created a solid back for the custom-made banquette seating. A wrought-iron room divider was added as artwork, creating a visual barrier between the two.

Despite the small size of the house, the designers were able to include a bespoke, hand-painted kitchen, which included a fridge, freezer, larder and wine store. The carcasses were made in green MDF with hand-painted exteriors and oak-veneered interiors. The under-stairs space was cleverly utilised to squeeze in a very small WC and laundry cupboard. All of these were disguised as part of the kitchen cabinet work. The choice of a soft blue adds to the calm atmosphere of the whole space.

When considering the soft furnishings the designers retained a simple palette, using natural fabrics with coloured velvet accents which complement the blue at the lower level. A combination of a retro ceiling light, table lamps and subtle lighting in the cooking space ensure that the lighting is well layered and complementary to the whole concept. A window seat with squab cushion makes use of the shallow bay window. By only having a dwarf cupboard and shelves on one side of the fireplace there is sufficient space for a desk on the other, making a peaceful space for anyone working from home.

Using window shutters rather than curtains or fabric blinds provides privacy without adding clutter to the simply decorated space.

OUTCOME

The sleek finish of the kitchen cupboards, and unobtrusive, subtle design details throughout the living space and kitchen add to the calm and sophisticated atmosphere in the space exactly as requested by the client.

FIGURE 1.21: The custom-designed screen and banquette are a neat device to create broken living spaces within the same room.

FIGURE 1.22: A calm and elegant sitting room is enhanced by natural fabrics and comfortable upholstery, while the custom joinery follows the same simple lines as the rest of the ground floor

FIGURE 1.23: A desk fitted between the fireplace and the new dwarf cupboards in the centre of the open-plan room create a practical workspace on the upper level.

2

....

THE COOKING SPACE

....

To design a kitchen of any size requires a combination of an enquiring mind, creative energy and military planning. There may be a temptation on the part of the designer to hand the entire process to a dedicated kitchen designer – but kitchens are fun to do, and exploring the possibilities with the client, resolving the challenges and seeing the end result makes them a rewarding exercise for all. The biggest challenge with a limited space will almost certainly be trying to fit too much into too small an area.

Manipulating the available space, trying to create more if possible, considering the overall look and then developing the different elements will take time and effort – inevitably more than originally expected. There will be clients whose idea of cooking is to rustle up some scrambled egg on a Sunday evening, while eating out most of the time, and others who love to cook, and want a design which fits their personal culinary style. The minimalist might want everything hidden when not in use, and the cosy kitchen afficionado may prefer a cottagey look, with a jumble of kitchenalia on display. There will be occasions when a small cooking area is part of a much larger multifunctional space, and other homes where the only place suitable for the kitchen is an area of barely three square metres. Working all of this out, being creative and including everything requested by the client requires a more clinical approach to design than in most areas of the home. A checklist will be the designer's most important tool, and it is better to keep referring to it than to realise as the design is signed off that there is nowhere to put the refuse bins or the tea towels.

FIGURES 2.1A, 2.1B AND 2.1C: Interior design by Spencer & Wedekind. Brackenbury, London, 2014. An industrial-style extension and bespoke Shaker cupboards make use of every inch of this West London kitchen/dining room.

Whether the kitchen is to be part of a refurbishment or new build, it is wise to first work through a lengthy list of questions with the client. The answers to some might be obvious, but asking both the more obscure and the self-evident questions can be a good icebreaker when establishing a relationship with a new client.

As part of the briefing process, the designer will have a series of high-level questions, gradually working their way down to the minutiae of day-to-day use of the kitchen.

The first list could be based on the following:

- What is the approximate budget? As every designer soon learns, clients do not like admitting exact figures, but by setting upper and lower parameters the designer can guide the client towards bespoke, semi-bespoke, high-end factory-built or mass-market kitchen units. The designer's knowledge of different appliance brands, hardware, flooring and lighting will also be vital in persuading the client to consider one price-point of goods over another. The designer should also have an idea of installation costs, and by involving the main contractor early in the process they can ensure that a realistic ballpark figure is included to cover this.

- Who will be doing the cooking? Even with a small space it is worth checking whether the client will cook themselves or will have a cook/housekeeper/occasional chef for special occasions. If the cooking space is largely used by others, the practicalities might outweigh the aesthetics. There will be clients who live in luxury apartments with small kitchens who have a full-time cook or housekeeper and never venture into the kitchen, but who also expect it to be efficiently run and provide excellent cuisine no matter how small it is. On the other hand, an eat-in kitchen where the client does the cooking will be a much more personal area of the home. If the cooking space is part of the living area, what other furniture has to fit in? In modern, open-plan living the cooking area may consist of one wall of appliances and an island with the eating, sitting and workspace all combined in one large room. Equally, an eat-in kitchen might include a two-person breakfast bar, or a bistro table tucked into a window embrasure.

- Who will be using the kitchen? This is not the same question as who will do the cooking. The household might consist of an elderly couple, a disabled person, a young family, teenagers, students, holidaymakers, working professionals, or a combination of all of them. Each group will have slightly differing needs from the kitchen and its set-up.

- How tall is the client, their family or the housekeeper? Someone who is six feet or over may be happy having tall top cupboards, whereas a smaller person will need everyday items to be more accessible.

- How many people will be cooked for on a daily basis, and will there be times when that increases considerably – Sunday lunches or Shabbat dinners, for example?

- Are there any religious dietary laws to be followed, such as kosher? It is not difficult to design a kosher kitchen, but fitting one into a confined space will be a challenge for the designer.

FIGURE 2.2: Interior design by Mairi Helena. Edinburgh, 2017. An attic dormer is the ideal place for a breakfast nook in this interior designer/photographer's Edinburgh kitchen.

FIGURES 2.3A, 2.3B AND 2.3C: Interior design by Mary Leslie. London, 2012. In this small kosher kitchen the position of the sinks was tightly regulated by the building's management committee, and the challenge of separating appliances, cooking equipment and food into *milch* and *fleisch* was solved by a diagonal walkway between the two areas and a single large refrigerator to serve both.

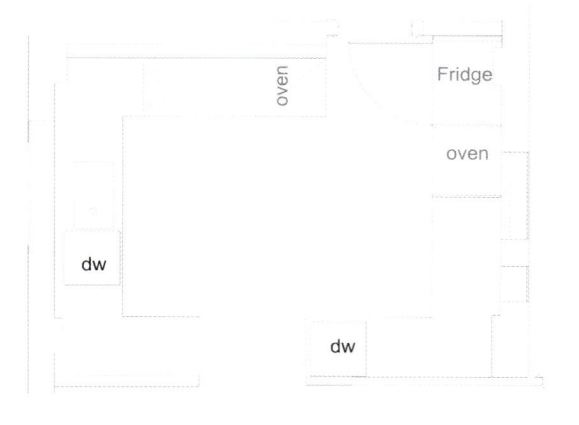

The designer should commission a full measured survey of the space at the beginning of the project, and from it work out whether improvements can be made to the internal layout by removing partitions, borrowing space from elsewhere, or extending the property. Relocating the kitchen completely might improve the flow of the entire house. If the project is a new build there will be scope for clever use of space, and the designer should be adept at finding extra room for cooking, storage and eating efficiently in whatever room is available. The architect and designer might have differing visions for the kitchen and other ancillary areas, which will need to be resolved amicably early on in the process. There are various advantages to integrating the kitchen with some of the living space, which the designer should discuss with the client.

If the kitchen is the heart of the home, the household and visitors can share in preparation, cooking and socialising around the cooking space and throughout the living area. With fewer walls there will be more natural light throughout the room. It will also be easier for parents to watch children at play or doing homework.

On the other hand, the designer and client might explore keeping a separate cooking space, which gives more privacy in the living area – more convenient if the latter is used as a workspace. Having a separate kitchen should also allow for more wall space in both kitchen and living room, which is useful when seeking room for shelves, cupboards and artwork.

Before working out where to put the pots and pans, there are a number of other practicalities to be included in the planning:

- In a refurbishment project, how will the contractors remove the old kitchen and bring in the new one? Is there a lift or a tight staircase, and are there restrictions on their use? It is possible that in a walk-up it will be necessary to use a cherry-picker to deliver the new kitchen. If it is bespoke, can some of it be assembled on site for ease of access?
- If the client is keen on upcycling, or the existing kitchen units only need a small amount of improvement, is there benefit in retaining some or all of them? New cupboard fronts on an old kitchen are the most cost-effective refresher. Can the rejects be recirculated in the community?
- Will the existing floor structure take the weight of the proposed units and appliances? Cast-iron range cookers in particular require a solid concrete base.

If the designer is using a main contractor for the project, but the kitchen is being built under separate contract, or no main contractor is employed and the designer is responsible for all the individual trades as project manager or coordinator, care must be taken that no trades and their costs fall between the different estimates. To avoid that situation, the lead designer or architect should explain in detail the phases of the project to the client, along with their benefits. Clients who are in business themselves should follow these with ease, but others might not understand the importance of defined contacts, agreed lines of communication, detailed estimates and a clear timeline. A wise designer will stand firm and ensure that the client has understood the phases and their implications at the start of the project. Clients who change their minds partway through the contract, who are swayed by comments from well-meaning friends without understanding the implications, or who decide to employ their own contractors for part of the work outside of the main contract need to understand that their changes will affect the cost and the whole carefully worked-out plan.

FIGURES 2.4A AND 2.4B: Architecture by Mary Arnold Forster Architects. Western Isles of Scotland, 2017. A sketch shows how the kitchen will relate to this open-plan new build. The result is stylish and discreet, with most paraphernalia stowed out of sight.

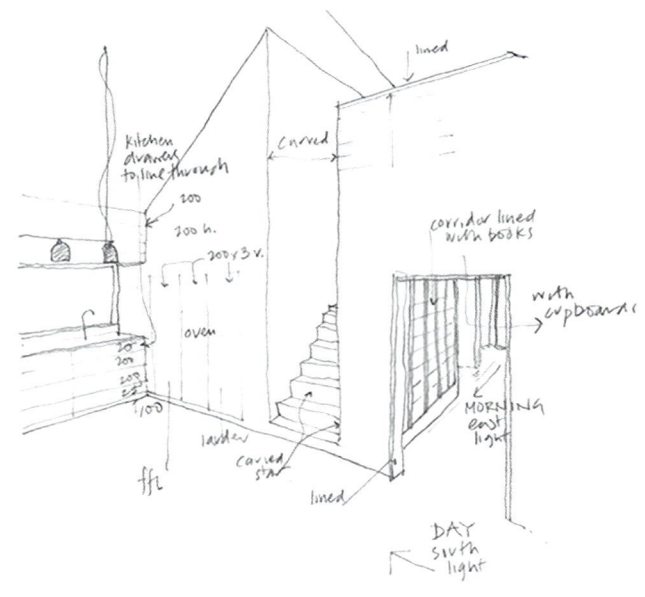

Even a compact kitchen will require detailed designs. These might start with freehand sketches or the designer standing in the available space, waving their arms around and sounding inspired. However, the designer needs to convert those bright ideas into CAD drawings, elevations, electrical layouts and, in a bespoke kitchen, the architectural details. All of that has to be costed into the fee structure at the outset, and the designer will soon find out that it will probably take twice as long as anticipated.

If the kitchen is to be hand-built, the designer needs to agree with the joinery company or main contractor what full-size shop drawings, or rods, will be provided, and at what point they will be available for inspection. The client needs to understand the importance of this process and the time it may take to carry out effectively. Many experienced designers can recount an occasion where the client took their designs, insisted that a local firm would do the project at half the price, the local firm then assured the client that inspecting the rods was not necessary, and the end result was wrong. Looking at the rods with the joiner, seeing the designs become reality, spotting any areas where there may be problems and resolving them together are part of the pleasure of design teamwork.

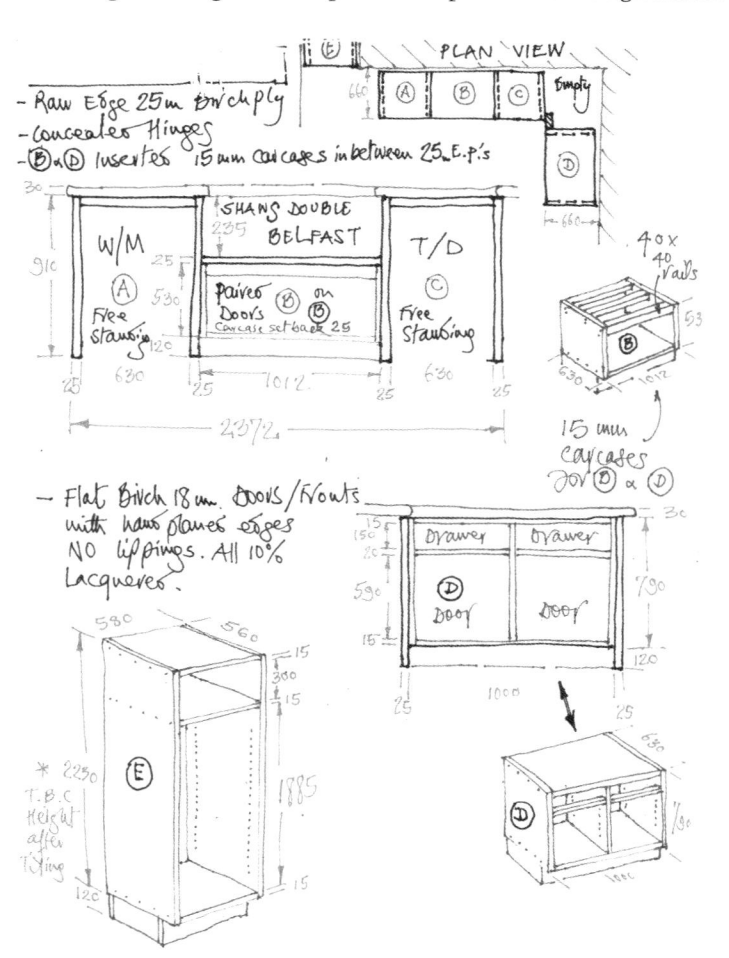

FIGURE 2.5: Interior design by Mary Leslie. Drawing by Geoff Jackson of Langley Furniture Works. Northumberland, 2019. Where the designer cannot visit the workshop to see full-size rods it is essential to check every detail with the manufacturer to avoid costly mistakes.

FIGURES 2.6A, 2.6B AND 2.6C (below): Interior design by Eva Byrne of Houseology. Dublin, 2019. Reworking the ground floor layout makes space for an elegant kitchen, laundry and bathroom. A simple floor plan (c) shows the best use of space in this Dublin cottage.

The final, and most important, high-level question has to be 'how would you like the kitchen to look?' A client who likes everything to be out of sight might want a linear, white, contemporary kitchen, or perhaps warm, rich natural timber. One who likes a cottage-style kitchen could have an unfitted space with random, old pieces of furniture squashed in together around a range. Some clients see their crockery and glass as ornaments to be on display, in which case floating shelves or glass-fronted cupboards are an easy solution. The soft furnishings; suitable floor finishes; walls which can be panelled, painted, tiled or papered; colour and texture can all be used to realise the client's dream.

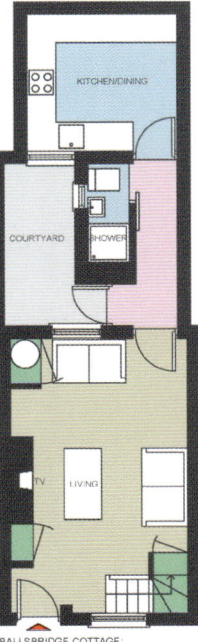

BALLSBRIDGE COTTAGE:
GROUND FLOOR PLAN - BEFORE

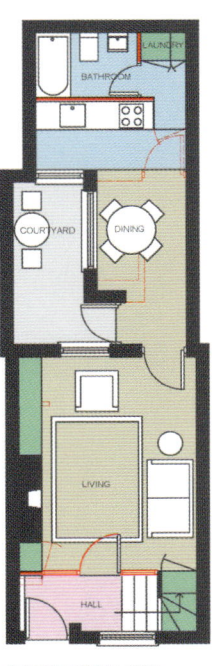

GROUND FLOOR PLAN - AFTER

Once the high-level questions have been answered, and the designer has an idea of the style of kitchen the client is looking for, a second set of questions need to be asked. These can be used to eliminate appliances or cooking utensils from the list that might be good to have, but for which there is no room in a confined space.

As mentioned earlier, all sorts of people might use the kitchen. Elderly or disabled members of the family might need flexible, low-level units, easily manipulated taps and bar handles. The designer should also consider safety if there are small children around. Can they reach the basics once they are old enough? Is the hob safe? If the hob is on a peninsula, this needs to be wide enough that pans do not poke out at the back.

When considering the look of the cooking space the client needs to choose work surfaces, splashbacks, and floor and wall finishes. A kitchen, even a small one, does not have to be light in colour, and a client who likes a moody, glamorous look might opt for a dark cooking space with plenty of black granite and reflective surfaces to match. A new build in timber might work well with pale tiled floors and oiled wood surfaces. Not everyone wants full splashbacks – the client might prefer a cooking space with no tiles at all. Industrial-style kitchens look good with stainless steel, polished concrete, and bare or painted brick combined with wood.

FIGURE 2.7: Design by Mary Arnold-Forster Architects. Iona, Scotland, 2020. An island hob should have plenty of space at the back to ensure that pans cannot be knocked over in passing.

Running through a list of appliances and gadgets with the client will focus the mind, particularly when small versions of important items such as dishwasher, oven and sink must be considered. Any item which can be multifunctional will help reduce the number of appliances the designer must squeeze in. This list might include:

- Hob – gas, electric, induction, range
- Oven/Microwave/Grill – for a very constricted space the designer can steer the client towards a multifunction oven, which performs all of these functions and can be a true space saver.
- Extractor – could be above, within or behind the hob. Is it to be a ducted or recirculation type?
- Sink – under-mounted, surface-mounted, multifunctional, single, 1½, double?
- Taps – with or without water filter or boiling water supply, some of which require extra space under the sink?
- Dishwasher – full-size, slimline, integrated?
- Fridge/Freezer – full-height, under-counter, integrated? Is there anywhere else on site such as an outhouse or utility room to put the deep freeze?
- Radiator, plinth heater, underfloor heating, air-conditioning – depending on available wall space, convenience and climate.
- Waste disposal unit
- Food processor/Food mixer – these, along with their attachments, take up a good deal of space either in the cupboard or on the worktop.
- Juicer
- Tabletop grill
- Toaster
- Kettle
- Integrated coffee machine

The designer and the client may now have agreed on a list of appliances which they hope to fit into the space, but where are they to put all the other eating and dining paraphernalia? The next list should include everyday cooking and eating items, such as:

- Crockery – how many place settings?
- Glassware – how many different sizes?
- Cooking knives – clients may prefer to have them in a drawer, in a worktop block or on wall-mounted magnetic strips.
- Other cooking utensils
- Chopping boards and trays
- Pots and pans, casserole dishes
- Roasting and baking tins and trays
- Weighing scales
- Tea towels
- Cleaning materials
- Foil, clingfilm, greaseproof paper, plastic bags
- Herbs and spices
- Food

FIGURE 2.8: Design by Eva Byrne of Houseology. Dublin, 2003. A semi-fitted industrial-style run of appliances makes best use of space in this open-plan new build.

Unless the client has a separate utility room or extra cupboard space, they are unlikely to have room for other gadgets such as ice-cream machines, bread makers and rice cookers. They may also need to add in a clothes washer/dryer in the absence of a laundry room.

The designer must then consider essential services such as the location of the water supply, waste disposal, recycling and refuse collection. Fortunately there are some very good, compact, pull-out recycling bins on the market. The location of the water supply and waste pipes will dictate the position of the sink, and the rest will flow around it.

By this stage the cooking area will be taking shape. Whether it is a small room or part of an open-plan space, the designer and client should have a good idea of what services will go where; however, a few more points need to be considered.

With the appliances roughly in place, the designer needs to discuss the electrical installation, including supply for the hob/oven/microwave and other appliances. There is an adage that a kitchen can't ever have enough power points, and it would be wise to include at least three double sockets for everyday use, and preferably more. The client might want an integrated USB socket and other media or IT sockets somewhere in the cooking space. Does the client want to have a flatscreen TV or computer screen on view? Are they having a sound system throughout the property, in which case they might want speakers in the ceiling? Is somewhere in the space the optimum position for the household wi-fi router?

FIGURE 2.9: Interior design by René Dekker. London, 2016. LED strips are used to good effect below the plinth and the top cupboards in a sleek Chelsea attic kitchen.

There are some interesting options for lighting depending on the size of the space. Starting with natural light, it might be possible to include a skylight or sun pipes to bring extra light into a dark space. With so many LED options to consider, the designer can layer the light by adding lighting below the plinths, above and below the worktop, above the cabinets, and inside glass-fronted cupboards. It is vital that there is enough light over any work surface, so if the cooking space includes a peninsula or island the designer needs to ensure that the cook can do their preparation and cooking without being caught in their own shadow. Pendant and rise and fall lights can be a practical and decorative feature over the work surface.

After so much discussion, the designer now faces the challenge of fitting everything into the available space. Ideally, they will be able to design a bespoke kitchen which will make use of every available millimetre. If this is the case, cabinets and drawers can be adjusted to fit awkward spaces and take advantage of extra height, which factory-built kitchens may not allow.

Taking cabinets right up to the ceiling allows extra storage for seldom-used items. The designer needs to be able to argue which is better in each instance – using the height for storage, or having lower cupboards with room above for lighting, which will bounce light off the ceiling and make the room feel more spacious and less enclosed. A clever device is to use a rail and ladder for access to very high cupboards rather than steps, as the ladder itself can be a decorative feature when not in use.

FIGURE 2.10: Interior design by Jo Bee Ltd. Yorkshire, 2019. Pendant lights can be both practical and fun.

One of the first theory lessons any designer will learn about planning a kitchen is the cooking triangle, with the idea being that anyone working between the three main areas (sink, fridge and cooker) should move around a triangle, and that anyone else coming into the cooking space should not interfere with that flow, particularly between hob and sink. To ensure this the designer should imagine preparing a meal step by step in the newly planned compact cooking space, drawing a line from place to place during the process. If the result is an approximate triangle the theory works. If it looks more like the travels of an adventurous worm there is too much movement around the kitchen, and this should be revised if possible. Even if the hob and oven are separated the designer should still avoid too much crossover of the lines during the cooking process. Good points to look for in the design are a place close by to put hot dishes when they come out of the oven, and avoiding the need to carry pans of boiling water across a pathway, particularly between hob and sink.

FIGURE 2.11A AND 2.11B: Interior design by Armstrong Keyworth. London, 2008. A basic work triangle is applied to ensure that this small kitchen functions efficiently, and the striking black units make it a stylish addition to a London designer's own home.

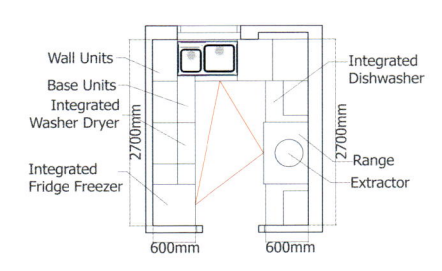

Most factory-built kitchen ranges are modular, so they do not offer the same flexibility; however, the better the range, the more variation in modules there will be. If the budget only allows for a mass-market kitchen the points to look out for are the quality of the door hinges and drawer runners, along with the structural integrity of the cabinets, particularly with flat-packed goods. The designer can also combine low-cost units with bespoke joinery to make the room more interesting.

At the end of the process the designer should have a cooking area which makes best use of the space, reflects the client's character and is a joy to work in, no matter how small it happens to be.

Checklist — have you asked the client:

- What are your priorities for the kitchen?
- What is your budget?
- Who is going to use the cooking space?
- Do you want it to be cut off from or part of the living space?
- What appliances would you like to include?
- How much crockery/cutlery/glassware would you like to show?
- How much food do you keep in the house?
- What balance of fridge/freezer space do you prefer?
- Are there pets?
- How would you like it to look?

FIGURE 2.12: Interior design by Benjamin Tindall Architects. East Lothian, Scotland, 2012. The essentials can fit into a tiny space if they need to.

DESIGNER   Benjamin Tindall Architects

CLIENTS   An academic couple in Edinburgh

BRIEF   The brief was to transform a dark and awkwardly shaped kitchen contained in a re-entrant angle on the top floor of an end-of-terrace Edinburgh tenement into a light, convenient and sociable space. The clients enjoy cooking and entertaining in a relaxed atmosphere. They wanted to be able to cook and talk, but keep the two areas separate, with plenty of opportunity to display their eclectic collection of artefacts and memorabilia.

LOCATION   A third-floor, end-of-terrace tenement flat in central Edinburgh.

CHALLENGES   The property is a good-sized flat, but not enough space was available for the kitchen/dining area, although both had to be contained within the existing envelope. The main problem was lack of natural light, with the existing sink in front of the only window, and the awkwardly shaped room leading to dark corners and no immediately obvious layout. The ceiling height also threw the room out of proportion.

A space had to be found for a full-height fridge/freezer which would not interfere with the sight lines, and a new position for the sink linked to the only existing external waste pipe on the corner of the property. A duct to

FIGURE 2.13

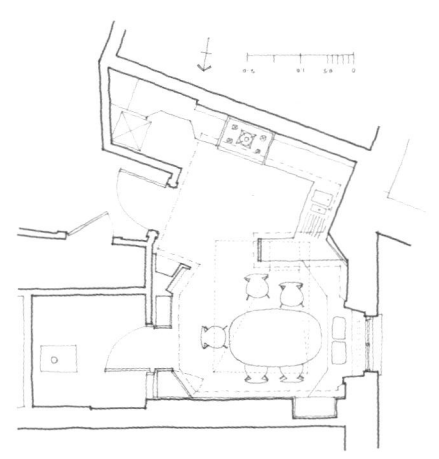

Figure 2.14: By moving the sink away from the window and reworking the space, a dark and awkward kitchen becomes two well-defined and complementary spaces.

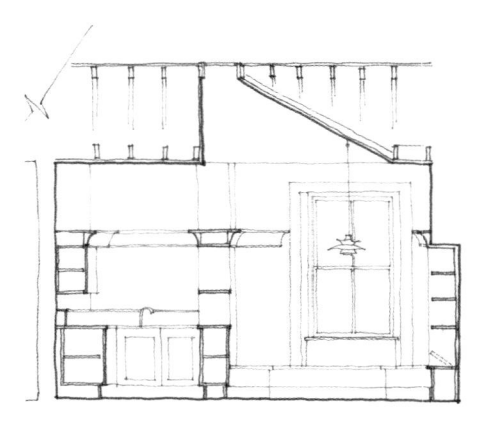

FIGURE 2.15: An architect's sketch shows how the new roof light adds natural daylight to the space, while the oversized cornice at a lower level draws the eye down and improves the proportions of the while room.

the atmosphere for the extractor over the hob also had to be considered, and routed away through the roof space above. There was only one door from the corridor to the room, with another leading to a walk-in cupboard, neither of which could be repositioned.

The architect reworked the space so that the dining and social area would be closest to the window, while the cooking space would be next to the kitchen door and defined by a bespoke room divider separating the two areas.

The ceiling was very high for the footprint of the room, so to improve the proportions he created an exaggerated cornice at low level around the new display units.

The new skylight was positioned in the only place possible, allowing for the valleys in the roof. The architect created a very geometric light shaft, skewed to bring natural light over the table.

By using ready-made oak kitchen units, the architect was able to save money within the budget, which could be used for the bespoke display shelves and cupboards. Setting the kitchen wall cupboards directly under the exaggerated cornice gives the impression that they are part of a more bespoke solution. The custom-made English slate worktop is pleasingly tactile and complements the gentle overall colour scheme. The linoleum floor is highly practical and deliberately does not detract from the overall design.

To light the two spaces, strips were used to light the shelves and the work top, while a classic Poul Henningsen Scandinavian lamp hangs over the dining table.

A further nod to Scandinavian design was intended for the dining table, which the team wanted to be super-elliptical; the perfect shape to seat six. The table shown here was temporary, while the clients searched for the perfect solution to accompany Arts and Crafts-style dining chairs from the Edward Barnsley Workshop.

The squab seat, cushions and curtains echo the simple Arts and Crafts feel of the space and soften the window nook without detracting from the subtle palette.

OUTCOME The clients were thrilled by the clever manipulation of space and new natural light provision, which created a kitchen modest in look, but not in standard.

FIGURE 2.16: The bespoke, exaggerated cornice shows to advantage above the plain oak cabinets. A sun pipe provides extra daylight for the cooking space and low-level strips ensure sufficient light over the work surfaces.

FIGURE 2.17: By moving the sink to one side the architect created a comfortable window nook to provide extra seating in the compact dining area, itself transformed by the new light shaft.

CASE STUDY 2.2: MARY LESLIE INTERIOR DESIGN

DESIGNER Mary Leslie

CLIENT A young City professional who was a first-time buyer

BRIEF The original brief was to give the client a comfortable, sophisticated home with a new kitchen to his exact specification. He was a keen cook and wanted to be sure that he could produce elegant dinner party food despite the size of the kitchen. He has always liked different woods and specifically requested a wooden rather than a painted or laminate finish.

The designer was also asked to create some form of laundry space and a new bathroom, all of which had to be fitted into the central section of the apartment.

FIGURE 2.18: Even the smallest of spaces can have a fine-looking kitchen.

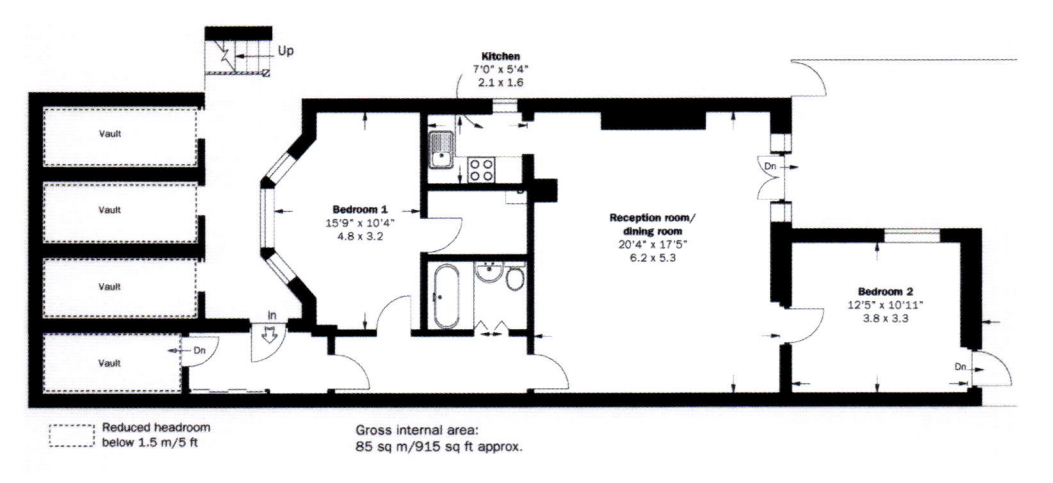

FIGURE 2.19: The floor plans illustrate the need to make best use of the three small central spaces.

LOCATION   A basement flat in London's Notting Hill

CHALLENGE   The apartment is in the basement of a five-storey Victorian end-of-
terrace house in London's Notting Hill. In the middle of the flat were
three small spaces: the kitchen (2.1 x 1.6m), a central space containing
the washing machine and boiler, and a tired shower room. The designer
hoped to incorporate the central space into the kitchen; however, a
quick conversation with a structural engineer confirmed that the walls
were supporting the four storeys above and there was no possibility of
knocking through between the kitchen and utility areas.

Left with the spaces as they were, the designer squeezed a bath with
overhead shower into the original shower room as requested by the client,
turned the central space into a utility room, and focused her attention on
the kitchen.

To maximise the space she decided on a bespoke kitchen, which could
have joinery of any size to ensure that every inch was used. A multipurpose
stainless-steel sink came with a chopping board which created a useful
work surface, and a slimline dishwasher was also squeezed in. Rather
than take the units up to the ceiling, the designer left a gap sufficient for
uplighting, which gave the illusion of raising the ceiling height. There was
very little floor area, and the client opted for vinyl as it would be easy to
maintain and hardwearing.

At only 1.6m wide, the kitchen had to be L-shaped. Fortunately there was
space under the window cill for a freestanding bin. The flat came with an
under-pavement vault, which left ample space for larger recycling bins.

Once the appliances had been fitted into the space, there was enough space for one small drawer pack and a limited number of cupboards. However, there was no room for the client's crockery, so the designer suggested a custom-made credenza for the living room to sit under the flatscreen TV, which would not only include the audiovisual components, but also had sections for the crockery and some other storage.

As the flat was end-of-terrace there was no problem with bringing deliveries along the side of the house and through the garden doors. It is vital for the designer to check beforehand that everything can be delivered to the property, and a luxury to have one as easy as this.

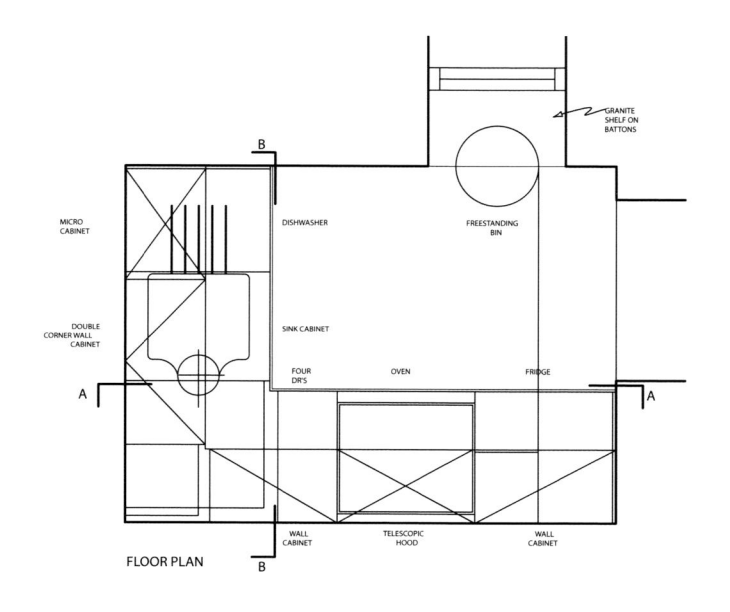

FIGURES 2.20A, 2.20B AND 2.20C: Every inch of space has to work in a small kitchen. Bespoke design is the best way to achieve this.

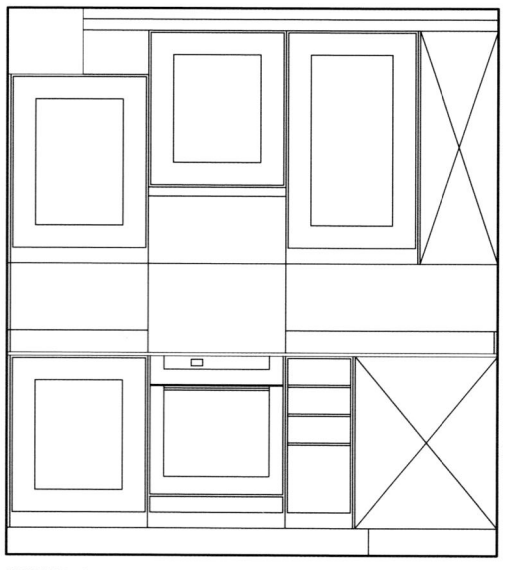

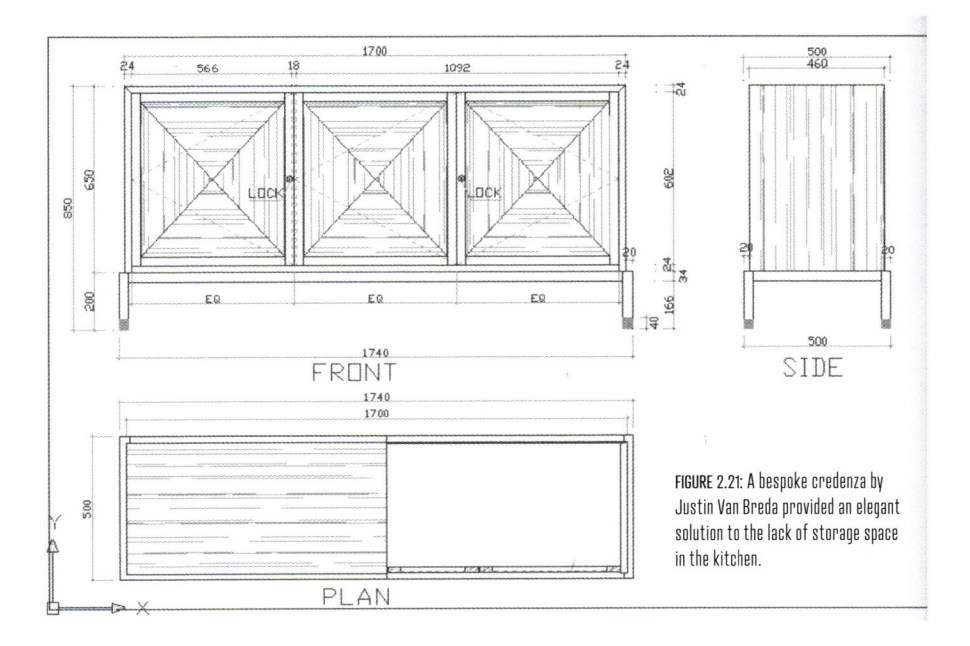

FRONT

SIDE

PLAN

FIGURE 2.21: A bespoke credenza by Justin Van Breda provided an elegant solution to the lack of storage space in the kitchen.

OUTCOME   The client was relieved to have a kitchen which fulfilled its purpose despite its size. The design meant that he could cook comfortably in it, and the overall look satisfied his love of wood and preference for a traditional look. The designer enjoyed working with someone only just discovering his personal design voice, and who was ready to invest in bespoke finishes which achieved the look he wanted.

FIGURE 2.22: Every kitchen needs a set of drawers, even if they are only 250mm wide.

CASE STUDY 2.3: JEFFREYS INTERIORS/PEDEN & PRINGLE

FIGURE 2.23: The banquette seat makes the dining area instantly inviting in this Edinburgh basement kitchen.

DESIGNERS   Kimberley Bremner, lead interior designer at Jeffreys Interiors, collaborated with Camilla Pringle, director at Peden & Pringle, who were responsible for the design, manufacture and installation of bespoke cabinetry throughout the house.

CLIENTS   A professional couple moving to Edinburgh with their two teenage children

BRIEF   The brief was fairly loose. Originally, the clients did not intend to change the existing kitchen; however, it soon became apparent that they needed more storage, and that a kitchen/dining room would enhance the limited space in the basement. After some discussion and various proposals, they agreed to strip out the existing units and refurbish the whole area. The budget was both flexible and realistic, with the most important aim being to find a style and layout which maximised the storage, allowed for family and friends to gather together, and fitted the overall design themes in the house.

LOCATION   A late-Georgian townhouse in Edinburgh's Stockbridge area

The challenges were considerable. The kitchen is in the original basement of a listed building, with very low ceilings and only accessed via a narrow staircase with a tight turn. There is no access to the basement through a front basement area or rear garden.

The original kitchen was on two different levels, with the breakfast area raised a step higher than the working space. The kitchen designers suggested levelling off the space, which would give a much better flow to the room. This involved digging out the platform with hand tools and laying a 300mm-deep concrete slab to create a new level floor throughout.

There were potential problems with delivering worktops, splashbacks and appliances to the basement without having to cut too many sections, which should be avoided on aesthetic grounds. No one wants to see worktop

FIGURE 2.24: The original kitchen was in good condition, but lacked storage space and had an awkward change of level between the cooking and dining areas.

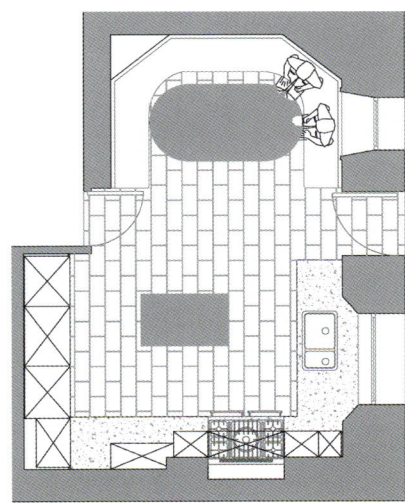

FIGURE 2.25: A simple floor plan shows how the redesigned kitchen has a new layout, which maximises available space while leaving plenty of room for friends and family to gather around the dining table.

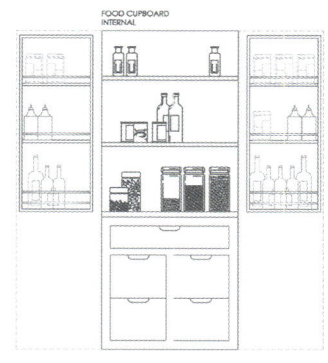

FIGURE 2.26: A meticulously designed larder cupboard provides much-needed storage space, which was lacking in the previous kitchen.

FIGURE 2.27: The bespoke dining table melds with the furniture in the rest of the house while precisely fitting the available space in the kitchen.

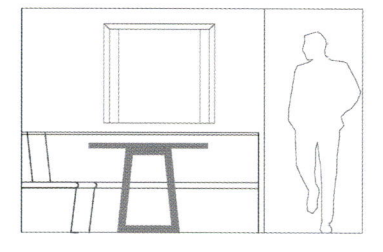

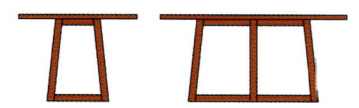

joins in the wrong place, which break up the continuity of finish. Most of the cabinetry was built in situ, as the cabinets were too large to deliver via the curved staircase. Appliances had to be chosen carefully to ensure that they would also fit down the stairs and through the basement door. As in many houses of this age and type, the ground and first floors appear to have generous proportions, but the basement and the attic, both the domain of servants, were built to be much tighter on space and light. The main contractors worked closely with Peden & Pringle to ensure that the installation went smoothly throughout despite the difficulties with access.

The designers took the cabinetry tight to the ceiling, so the room felt higher, which drew the eye line up and opened up the space. One family member is a keen baker, and the broad wooden work surface on the island combined with the bank of cupboards to one side created an excellent relationship between food preparation or service, and safe movement around the kitchen.

The dining area, with its wraparound banquette and custom-made dining table, disguised the awkwardly shaped space and ensured a free cooking zone and passage from staircase to garden.

The clients were absent for much of the project, and only met the team from Peden & Pringle briefly at the start of the project. Efficient electronic communication was key to the smooth running of the process between the clients, designers, main contractor and specialist cabinetmakers.

Colours throughout the house are bold, with plenty of pattern and texture. The designers chose to paint the units in Studio Green, with the larger cupboard interior finished in matt oiled oak. It is acknowledged that a dark room does not necessarily become light by painting it a light colour; here the colour contributes to the overall atmosphere of the space, which is exactly as the clients hoped.

OUTCOME While the clients thought they liked the existing kitchen, they were thrilled by the new one. The revised layout, with its focus on comfort, convenience and attention to detail, ensured that every inch counted and resulted in a room where the whole family can cook, eat, relax and be together. As a result, the room is truly the hub of the home.

FIGURE 2.28: The moody dark green cabinets, dark stone floor, brass handles and oak-lined cupboards all add to the kitchen's grown-up atmosphere.

3

THE SLEEPING SPACE

Designing a bedroom is an intimate exercise, so the designer needs to keep the conversation especially relaxed when discussing the sleeping space – probably more than for any other space in the house. Ideally, the designer has already explained how it is necessary to 'climb inside' their clients' lives to create a genuinely bespoke interior. Even if the project involves a one-bedroom flat with limited options, plenty of questions need to be asked to make the best of the space. For many people, the place where they sleep will have been appropriated for other purposes, especially in a compact home. It is very likely that a sleeping space will also be the dressing room, with its wardrobes and so on; a workspace for teenagers and students; a play area for children; or a bedsitting room for an elderly relative. However, as we are constantly being urged to clear things out of the bedroom to allow for a good night's sleep, the first exercise should be to determine which of these can be moved elsewhere, and which are essential.

The designer can also turn that idea around, and ask how many of the functions in the home can be combined with the sleeping space. Might it also include plenty of storage, or a workspace, play area, music room or sitting room? Is the ceiling high enough to include a platform, bunk beds or even a mezzanine level? Would it work to have a bath in the bedroom and a very small space for a WC and basin elsewhere? All of these possibilities mean that the designer will have to explore options and alternatives with the client with tact and sensitivity.

The main limitation when contemplating the design will be the footprint of the room, followed by the height. The most basic bedroom contains a bed, one or two bedside tables, bedside lights, perhaps a chest of drawers, a chair, somewhere to hang clothes, and presumably a window on to the outside world. Within that box a combination of clever joinery, furnishings and decoration will be vital to reflect the character of the occupant. Older properties, especially cottages, tend to have (or had) more single bedrooms than new builds, and these work very well for children. When looking at the shape and size of some 'affordable housing' units it is questionable that it will be possible to include a double bed, a bedside table and be able to open the wardrobe door at the same time in what are, supposedly, double bedrooms. Odd shapes, sloping ceilings and doors in difficult places will often be found in smaller properties. The minor bedrooms of a large house can be equally tricky to furnish, and sloping ceilings again, large windows in narrow bedrooms, awkward pipes and inconveniently placed radiators are all likely to present challenges for the designer.

The most important aspect of a bedroom is that it feels comfortable and inviting. Much of that is achieved through personal possessions, furnishings and accessories. However, the designer's skill will be demonstrated by playing with scale and shape in order to fit everything into a small space. That might be by

FIGURE 3.1: Interior design by Spencer & Wedekind. Ravenscourt Park, London, 2018. Small rooms and unusual angles can be enhanced by bold wallpaper, such as in this attic bedroom.

59

CHAPTER 3   THE SLEEPING SPACE

opening up between rooms where possible, using height to fit in platforms, bunks and mezzanines, or more radically changing the layout of the property. During the briefing stage the designer must establish the client's routine and their storage requirements. A starting point for questions to the client might be:

On the bed and its surroundings:

- Who sleeps on which side?
- Do you like to read in bed, and what is your lighting preference?
- What kind of bed? (Size, which will likely be dictated by the room size, followed by bed type – divan base/bedstead/truckle/bunks/storage?)
- Do you want a TV in the bedroom? What other audiovisual requirements do you have?
- Do you prefer to do your makeup/grooming in the bedroom or bathroom? If in the bedroom, sitting or standing?

On clothes storage:

- Is there anywhere else we can put the clothes? (Is there room for a walk-in wardrobe or separate dressing area?)
- If the wardrobe has to be in the bedroom, would you prefer freestanding or built-in?
- Do you hang or fold your shirts and blouses?
- Do you prefer shoe rails, or space to stack shoe boxes?
- Do you have any preference about the way you hang trousers, suits, jackets and ties?
- How much space do you need for long and short dresses, occasion wear and coats?
- Will you need space for handbags and hats?
- Where do you like a full-length mirror?
- Do you like to swap winter and summer wardrobes, and store one while wearing the other – and if so, where shall we put the stored clothes?
- Do you need a safe, and if so, where would you prefer to put it?

FIGURE 3.2A: Interior design by Spencer & Wedekind. Ravenscourt Park, London, 2018. Upcycling a vintage draper's cupboard gives character to this practical dressing room.

FIGURE 3.2B: Interior design by Spencer & Wedekind. Ravenscourt Park, London, 2018. A jib door wrapped in wallpaper neatly hides the dressing room from sight.

Clever furniture layouts within the original footprint can also help. The standard one bed, two bedside tables layout tends to be symmetrical, but why? If a bed has to be fitted under eaves it may be more effective to set out the furniture askew. There will be those who object to having a bed in front of a window, but often the window is on the longest wall, and it may be the best or only place for it. If the room is very narrow, perhaps a floating shelf on each side of the bed will be sufficient for a bedside table.

Any designer who has worked on or lived in a period terraced house will be familiar with the fireplace and two alcoves scenario, where it makes sense to have a wardrobe on each side of the chimney breast. If the wardrobes are built

out from the alcoves, the bed may fit between them. In that case there will be no room for bedside tables, but niches within the wardrobe on either side of the bed can suffice. If the designer has managed to find a home for clothes elsewhere and the alcoves are shallow, they allow for good-sized bookshelves. A bed on a chimney breast without filling the alcoves in some form looks odd, and bedside tables in front of bookcases can be a good-looking and decorative solution. When setting out the floor plan using alcoves in this way, the designer must ensure that there is room to tuck in bedding on either side of the bed.

FIGURE 3.3 (below): Architecture by Darren Oldfield, interior design by Beth Dadswell. London, 2019. An alcove containing a bed needs to allow space for bedding and pillows — never just the width of the bed.

FIGURE 3.4 (right): Interior design by Eva Byrne. Ballsbridge, Dublin, 2019. A set of shelves can easily take the place of bedside tables in a tight space.

When discussing the type of bed for a property with limited storage, it is worth considering an ottoman divan base or wooden bed frame with built-in drawers, although in a limited space sharp corners on the bed end may cause too many barked shins for comfort.

For children's rooms, bunk beds can be fun. For the client on a limited budget there are some excellent sets of bunk beds available from furniture warehouses and department stores. However, as with most interior design, it is when the designer and client explore bespoke designs that real fun can be had.

There are a few points to consider when using ready-made bunks or platform beds. Crucially, will the frame fit the room? Oversizing the bed is an easy mistake to make. The bed dimensions may not take into account bolts or other fixings, and if the bunks are to fit into an alcove the designer needs to be sure that it will be possible to ease the frame into the space. Is there sufficient room for plugs or wires to run down at the back or side of the bed, and if the designer is planning surface wiring, will it be safe? Will the frame interfere with existing sockets and switches?

Bespoke bunks and platform beds will fit the available space exactly and use every inch to create something useful, unusual or amusing. The platform or bottom bunk can be built over storage such as pull-out drawers, or used to conceal a truckle bed for the occasional sleepover. Space on either end of the bunks could be used for bookshelves, hanging space or drawers. Allowing for headroom, any more space above the top bunk could be used to create a canopy. If the room permits the bunks can be built out from the wall to accommodate shelves along the back, providing useful extra space to display books, toys and trinkets.

FIGURE 3.5: Interior design by 2LG Studio. London, 2013. A built-in bed with storage drawers and funky decoration makes the most of this compact teenage bedroom.

FIGURE 3.6: Interior design by HÁM Interiors. Devon, 2001. Bunks, a reading nook and under-bed storage exploit the ceiling height in this small Devon bedroom.

Generally, bunks will be for children, so themes are a great way to make them fun. Pirate ships, trains, Wendy houses, tents and the like can all be used to give children their own special place. Custom-made bunks can accommodate good reading light and, depending on the target age group, sockets for USB chargers or night lights. The traditional two-bunk design is fine, but could you fit in three or four? Can you create nooks and crannies, or a reading space, or a mini study under the bed? If you are designing a holiday home where a crowd of people need beds, the bunks can be made comfortable for anyone.

If the sleeping space is intended for an occasional guest, sofa beds, wall beds and truckle beds can all be considered. Even a two-seat sofa which can be squeezed into a study or small sitting room gives space for the occasional guest. It is important to check the bed width against the sofa width, as arms and the frame take up a fair bit of space.

A drop-down bed within fitted bookshelves or cupboards can be a convenient way of creating space during the day. It is important when planning any kind of hidden bed to consider the bedding at the same time. Duvets, sheets and pillows all take up valuable storage space.

Studio or truckle beds are very useful, particularly in children's rooms where they can be used for sleepovers. If there is room in a study for a day bed set against one wall this can easily house a second bed underneath, making twin beds or a small double without occupying too much space day to day.

FIGURE 3.8: Interior design by Mary Leslie. London, 2004. If fitting a day bed into a study, there needs to be room to store the bedding — here it is in the bin at the end of the bed.

FIGURE 3.7: Interior design by HÁM Interiors. Devon, 2001. Cleverly positioned bunks can suit children or adults in this delightful seaside home.

If there are sloping ceilings, the design must ensure that any occupants will be able to get into bed without cricking their necks or banging their heads.

It might be that the client has a comfortable bedroom, but wants to store as many clothes as possible elsewhere. That is when a dressing room, walk-in wardrobe or corridor lined with storage will come in to play. These areas can also be small, but moving the clothes away from the sleeping space will make it much calmer and more conducive to rest and relaxation. Hopefully the designer and the client have already decided how much space is required for each group of clothes. It is likely that the client will want to store more than the designer can find the space to accommodate. However, clever manipulation of the space can achieve a surprising amount of storage in a small area.

The economy wardrobe can be constructed from baskets, rails and shelves bought in a DIY store. There are versatile possibilities in using chrome tubing with ball joints fixed from floor to ceiling and with rails at the required heights. However the best dressing room, like the best wardrobe, will be bespoke.

As a general rule, when planning the layout the designer should allow at least 600mm depth for the hanging space. A man's shirt will require approximately 1100mm from the top of the hanging rail, a skirt or pair of ladies' trousers about 1200mm, and a long dress as much as 1800mm. Every client will have different needs, but these figures are a starting point. Clothes need room to breathe; the closer together they are, the more crushed and the fustier they will become.

Once the hanging space has been calculated, the designer needs to squeeze in shelves, drawers, shoe and rails, and any other quirks requested by the client. Shoe drawers under the hanging space are a neat solution for the tidy client. The so-called hat shelf above may also be deep enough to take suitcases. All through the process the designer must consider the amount of space the joinery will take up. Just as in a kitchen, drawer slides, frames, carcasses and the fixed elements which give the whole design structural integrity all have to be taken into account. The doors could be sliding rather than fully opening, which makes for easier access, and glass is thinner than timber. In a confined space every centimetre has to work.

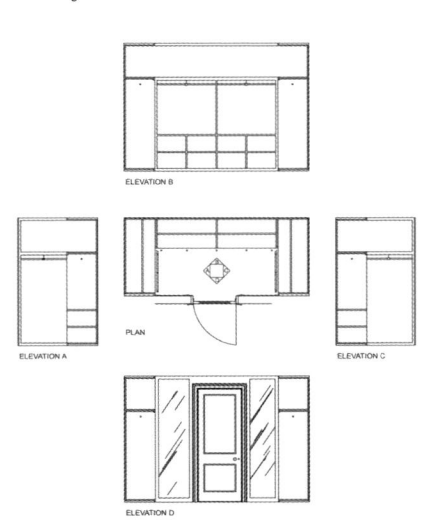

FIGURE 3.9: Interior design by Mary Leslie. London, 2012. These scale drawings show the client precisely how much space she has in reality — less than she thought.

FIGURE 3.10: Interior design by Mary Leslie. London, 2009. This small spare bedroom has modern shop fittings in place of a wardrobe – ideal for occasional guests.

For a guest bedroom the designer might query whether a wardrobe is necessary. These days plenty of people do not unpack if they are only staying a couple of nights, and do not need much hanging space except for the occasional dress or jacket. It might be worth looking at shop fittings, a row of hooks or a bentwood coat stand instead. Then the most important surface will be the one to put the bag or suitcase on; perhaps a bench with space for shoes below.

The type of flooring you have will very much depend on where you are in the world. In hot climates the floors will probably be tiled with the occasional mat or rug, avoiding wool if possible. In many places it is fashionable to have wooden floors, again providing the opportunity for a collection of rugs on the floor. However anyone who lives in a draughty old house, or who likes to pad about barefoot on a soft surface, will usually opt for carpet. Carpet also makes for a quieter room, which will generally be appreciated in a bedroom. A dressing room or walk-in wardrobe will be easier to maintain with a hard floor. That might be wood or tile, but it could also be leather, which gives a yielding surface, is easy on the foot, good-looking and durable. Underfloor heating is worth considering for a new build, or a client with an accommodating budget, but the designer should be conversant with the technical considerations of retrofitting both wet and dry systems before suggesting it to the client.

The basic idea of lighting a small bedroom is similar to lighting any size of bedroom. You will need good lighting by the bed, lighting for makeup and grooming, overhead light for cleaning, and a light on front of or inside the wardrobe if the client requires it.

A bedside light needs to be tall enough that someone can read while sitting up in bed, but not so obtrusive that it disturbs another person. The contemporary flexible lights which fix either to the headboard or to the side of the bed are useful here. They, and their more traditional swingarm counterparts, give flexibility. Tall, skinny lights or jointed desk lights can work too. The lamps to avoid are small and squat, which mean the light is too low for reading in comfort, or so chunky that the lamp sits away from the bed. Dimmers are wise in a bedroom, so that someone ill or resting can have low light; turned up, they give plenty of light for packing, sorting or cleaning. Even in a small bedroom the designer should give thought to the switching, and where possible have bedside lights and the overhead light switched from both door and bedside. The lights for makeup or grooming, which might be on a dressing table, chest of drawers or desk, need to be bright enough to light the face from both sides. The designer should avoid overhead lighting here, as it throws light down the face and this is never complimentary.

If the client has a bank of built-in wardrobes in the bedroom, it should be possible to light them inside, using either touch latches or an architrave switch. It is important that the lamp colour here gives an accurate reading of white. A client might have ten white shirts, each a slightly different shade, and they need to be able to pick the right one at a glance. If space permits (or in a walk-in wardrobe/dressing room) it should be possible to use downlights, but it is vital to check the elevations and section to make sure that the light is thrown down on to the garments and does not simply light the hat shelf. Where budget permits, even in a very small space, LED strips can be used to great effect to light different areas and make the wardrobe more interesting.

The overhead lighting could be a single, simple lampshade, a small chandelier or downlights over the bed. Directional downlights focused above the headboard also offer a layer of interest.

FIGURE 3.11: Interior design by Spencer & Wedekind. Ravenscourt Park, London, 2018. A wall-mounted desk light ensures comfort for work or reading in this attic bedroom.

FIGURE 3.12: Interior design by Benjamin Tindall Architects — Blue Cabin by the Sea. East Lothian, Scotland, 2012. Simple bedding and well-positioned reading lights ensure that this box bed will be comfortable for two adult guests.

FIGURE 3.13: Interior design by Spencer & Wedekind. Ravenscourt Park, London, 2018. Even in a small spare bedroom there is space for a bedside table balanced by wall lights high enough to make reading easy.

The bed is a major cost for anyone decorating a bedroom, and the designer should insist that the client try several. That means lying on them exactly as they would at home, moving around and trying to relax. From there, headboards, bed valances or dust ruffles versus upholstered bases and bedsteads are all a matter of personal choice. In a small room the bed needs the lightest of bedspreads, if any – otherwise they are an extra burden on limited storage. Bedside tables or shelves will ideally to be large enough to contain lamp, book, clock or radio, phone or tablet and tissue box – a few minutes deciding what each person likes to have beside them is time well spent. If the room is a guest bedroom there should still be space for most of these items.

If the bedroom is a bedsit or a retreat for an elderly person, it will need a comfortable armchair. The chair does not need to be large, but ideally it should be high-backed. Most people like somewhere to throw clothes temporarily, and the chair will be ideal. Any other furniture will be a matter of space – the style will already be a reflection of the client's taste and the designer's brief.

Checklist – have you asked the client:

- For each bedroom: who will be using the room?
- Will it just be a bedroom, or will it have other functions?
- How old are the occupants?
- What is the daily routine of getting up and going to bed?
- How do you like to arrange your bed and its surrounds?
- How do you like to organise your clothes storage?
- Do you have a colour preference for the room, or perhaps a scheme to avoid?

FIGURE 3.14: Interior design by Chris Dyson. London, 2010. However tight the sleeping space, it should be somewhere you want to linger.

CASE STUDY 3.1: MARY LESLIE INTERIOR DESIGN

FIGURE 3.15: The designer's challenge is to instil character into a new build with clever design and decoration.

DESIGNER	Mary Leslie
CLIENTS	A retired Anglo-American couple
BRIEF	New build apartments can be on the featureless side, with low ceilings, and not-quite-large-enough rooms. Developers aiming to maximise profit may not look at the design or layout in terms of the optimum convenience of the end user. The brief on this occasion was to improve the master bedroom in a riverside penthouse flat built in the early noughties. The clients were downsizing from a family home in the country to a lock-and-leave flat on the Thames, and requested individual wardrobes for their heavily edited clothes, as well as a comfortable seating area so that one could read on the sofa while the other sat up in bed for early morning tea. The latter point shows how important it is to talk through a client's daily routine in detail in order to make a room truly bespoke. The available room space allowed for summer or winter wardrobes but not both, with the remainder of the clothes being stored in a newly created walk-in cupboard carved out of the spare bedroom.
	Both clients had a love of fine joinery, which meant that they were open to a bespoke solution. They had high expectations for the final result and were prepared to pay attention to every detail in order to achieve their goal of simplicity and elegance in a property which would be their home for half of each year.
LOCATION	Overlooking the Thames in West London

As the clients were keen to have an interesting wood veneer for the wardrobe run and had already used cherry in the living room and beech in the study, it felt right to use maple in the bedroom. The harlequin design in opposing veneers broke up an otherwise linear unit, and was one of their favourite design devices in the flat.

The wardrobe interiors were tailored to suit each client, down to the position of shoe rails for his shoe size and the length of hanging for her blouses and dresses. Such attention to detail is vital to ensure that a wardrobe works. Lined in plain maple veneer, they were simple, elegant and functional.

The custom-made banquette seat between the cupboards allowed for a comfortable reading nook, with traditional swing-arm lights set into the wardrobe sides to complete the look.

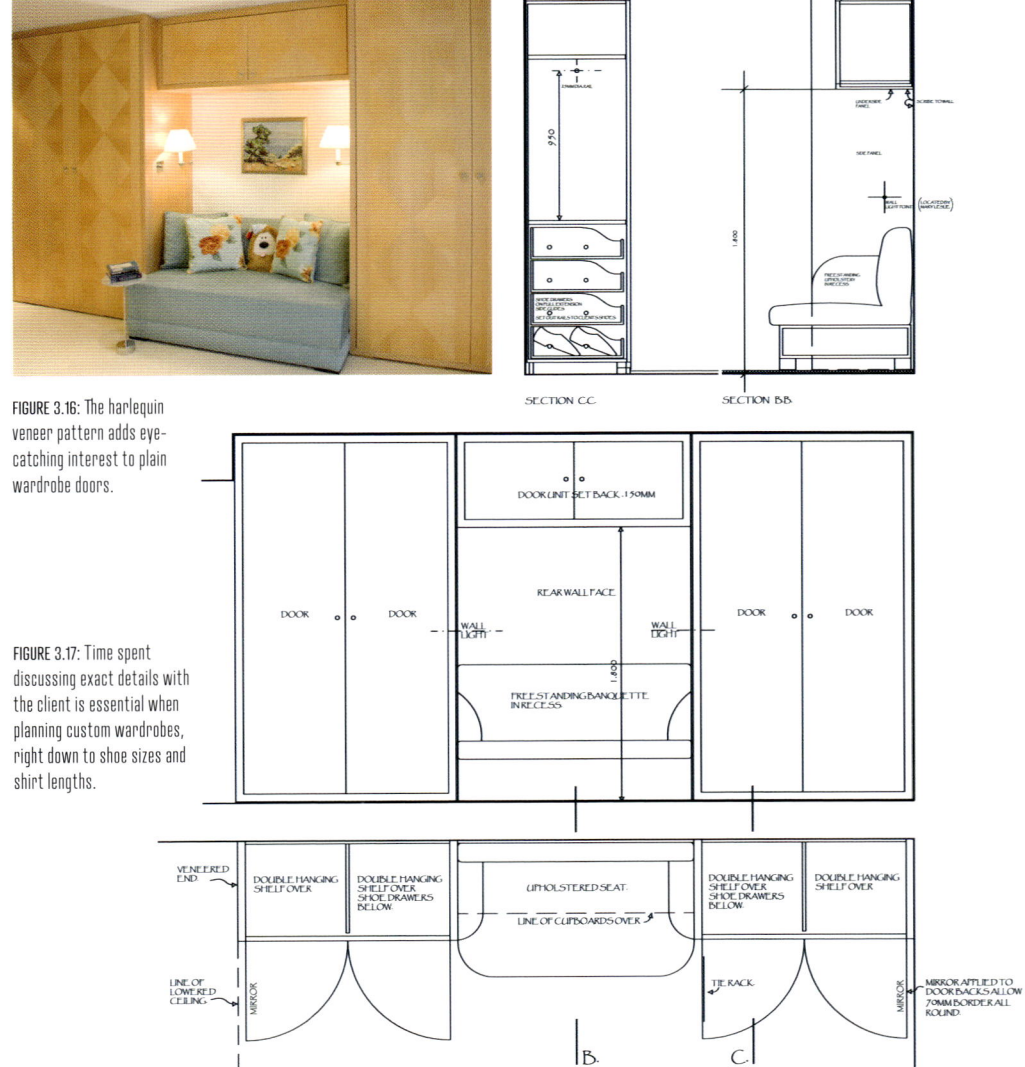

FIGURE 3.16: The harlequin veneer pattern adds eye-catching interest to plain wardrobe doors.

FIGURE 3.17: Time spent discussing exact details with the client is essential when planning custom wardrobes, right down to shoe sizes and shirt lengths.

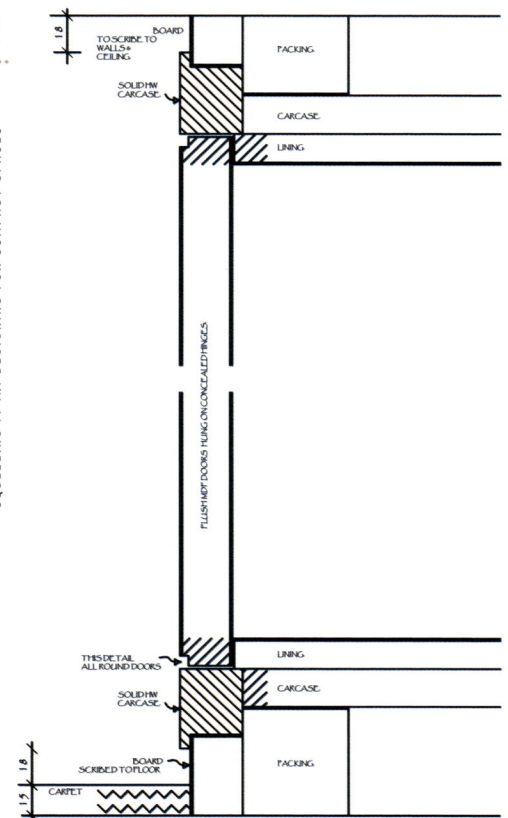

FIGURE 3.18: Allowing a flash gap around the tops of the wardrobes, and considering the depth and tog value of the carpet and ventilation are all details to be considered before signing off on the design.

Figure 3.19: Custom furniture design is as important as the joinery. This art deco-inspired parchment dressing table and William Yeoward side chair complement the overall scheme without distracting from the feature wardrobes.

The colour scheme was dictated by the appliqué wall-hanging of Scotland, which fitted perfectly above the bed. The clients had specifically requested heavy curtains and, along with the linen sheers, these gave the clients privacy and warmth while also disguising the rather tricky V-shaped windows. Many newbuilt flats have little or no deadlight for valances or pelmets, so in this case the designer used a covered lathe and fascia to ensure that no light would leak out of the top of the curtains. The scheme was complemented by a pair of custom-made walnut and nickel chests of drawers by William Yeoward, and a parchment-clad dressing table (affectionately referred to as 'the heirloom piece') from Renwick and Clarke.

OUTCOME

By removing the developers' built-in wardrobe and providing a bespoke solution the clients were given the aesthetic they hoped for, the storage they needed and the comfort they sought for every aspect of their retirement.

CASE STUDY 3.2: SPENCER & WEDEKIND

DESIGNERS   Spencer & Wedekind

CLIENTS   An Anglo-French professional couple

BRIEF   The property was an ugly duckling which had to be turned into a swan. The small Victorian terraced cottage was close to being condemned when the team first saw it. As with the ground floor (seen in case study 1.2), the clients wanted to renovate the house fully while recycling or restoring the existing materials where possible, to reflect their personal lifestyle and ethos. They hoped to have two bedrooms and a comfortable bathroom on the first floor without extending the property.

The clients wanted a serene and sophisticated master bedroom to continue the tailored and elegant look they sought for the ground floor. The bedroom also had to contain plenty of storage space. The brief was very specific about the layout of the wardrobes and other storage, which is reflected in the attention to detail in the wardrobes.

LOCATION   West London

FIGURE 3.20: Walnut display shelves and dwarf cupboards provide a well-proportioned frame for Adam Bell's charcoal-on-paper drawing, *The Living Other*.

The house was very run-down when the clients first found it, and the whole site had to be fully restored, including all-new joinery. Blown plaster, out-of-date plumbing and electrics, lack of central heating and unsafe floors meant the whole house was close to being condemned.

Happily, the designers and the clients were prepared to do what was necessary to make a contemporary home sympathetic to the original building.

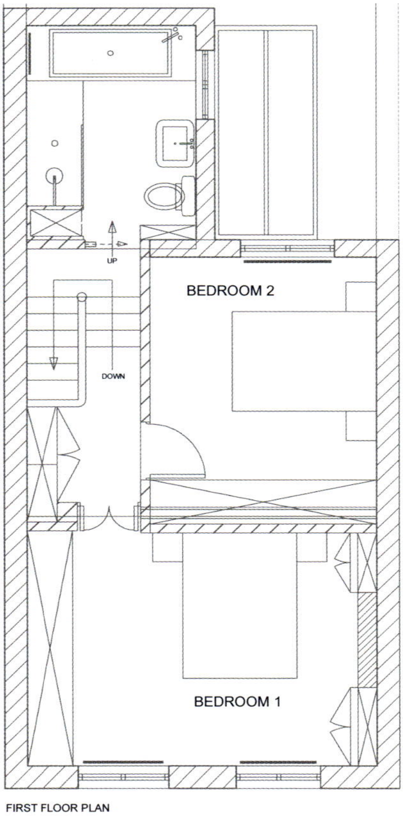

The designers were able to manipulate the space and, with a new stud partition between the two bedrooms and the landing, they could accommodate a full bank of wardrobes in the master bedroom and the same in bedroom two to provide much-needed wardrobe space. In this instance it was not possible to provide en-suite bathrooms for either bedroom.

The wardrobes carried the full depth of the main bedroom, and by using a small plinth and flash gap the designers were able to exploit the full height of the low-ceilinged room. They added panelling to both ceiling and walls to give visual interest to the flat planes of the space. As the building was a simple, Victorian artisan's cottage, it did not have any original cornices on the first floor.

The design of the chimney breast wall was also integral to the room. The low-level cupboards, some of which were very shallow, provided a base for display shelves.

FIRST FLOOR PLAN

FIGURE 3.21: The floor plan shows how tight the space was for the two bedrooms and their banks of wardrobes.

An industrial-style copper-lined wall light is an imaginative addition to highlight Adam Bell's artwork. Moving the partition wall between the two bedrooms meant that the alcoves either side of the chimney breast were no longer symmetrical; however, careful calculation of the geometry compensates for any inequality.

The clients wanted to be able to have a deep sleep, in blue serenity, and that is exactly what is achieved by this sophisticated design.

FIGURES 3.22A, 3.22B AND 3.22C: The birch ply interiors are meticulously detailed, and the plain bronze handles do not detract from the simplicity of the wardrobe doors.

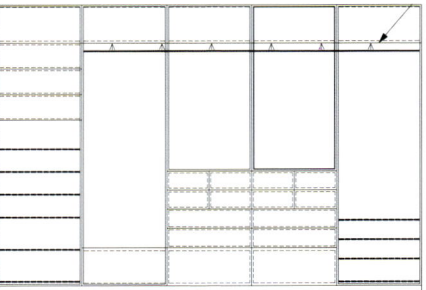

FRONT ELEVATION - INTERIOR

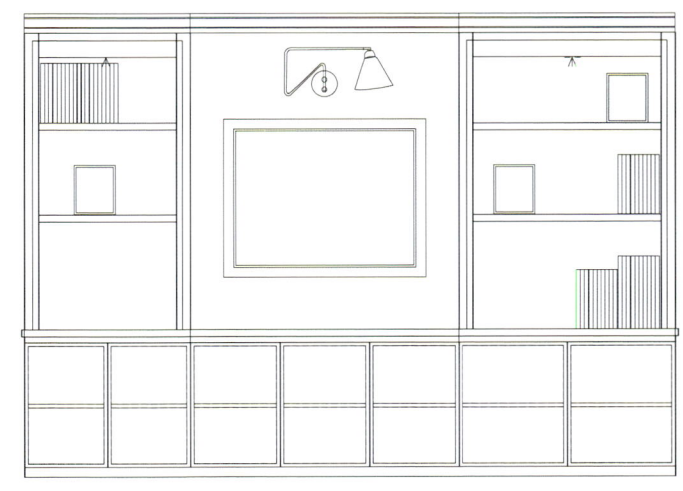

FRONT ELEVATION - INTERIOR

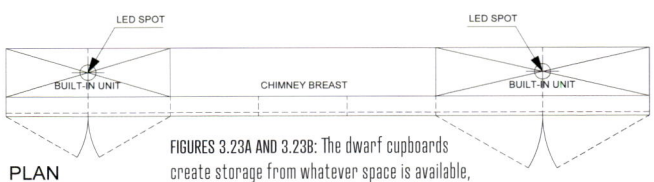

PLAN

FIGURES 3.23A AND 3.23B: The dwarf cupboards create storage from whatever space is available, and the polished solid walnut shelves and cupboard tops provide textural contrast against the serene blue of the walls and cupboards.

FIGURE 3.24: A close-up of the dwarf cupboards shows the careful detailing of the fake drawer fronts and subtle wall panelling in the master bedroom.

4

················

THE WORK SPACE

················

When wrestling with the lack of space in a small home, it can be tempting to assume that anyone working from a laptop will be happy sitting on the living room sofa or at the breakfast bar. However, it is likely that a home worker will need more room than a corner of the dining table. The more information the designer can glean about the client's needs, the easier it will be to decide where in the home to fit a suitable workspace. The first task is to find out what type of space the client needs.

When sounding out clients about their requirements, it is important to establish from the outset whether they only want somewhere to do personal administrative tasks, or whether they will be carrying out their actual work at home – in which case, the designer will need to find out what their occupation is, how much time they spend at home working on it, and whether they will be working alone or with others. It is also useful to know whether their own clients and customers will come to the home, or whether meetings will happen elsewhere. A farming, equine or canine set-up will generally involve meeting clients and sales reps at the kitchen table; however, others might be more formally entertained in the sitting room or outside the home.

Once the designer has established these basic facts, they should progress to the amount of space, equipment and services the client might need.

The minimum needed for any kind of work from a home environment is probably a laptop, but there will still be stationery and a printer to consider, so in practice almost everyone working from a laptop needs at least some dedicated space. A simple white desk, perhaps with a couple of bookshelves, always looks good, and may suffice not only for the laptop-based worker, but also for school homework or for everyday household admin. It can be stylishly dressed with accessories and personal effects, and it also works for those on a tight budget.

However, when trying to find room for working in a compact space it will most likely be better to create a bespoke area which accommodates the client and demonstrates the designer's skill.

Although some home workers will only need a laptop as described, most computer-based home workers prefer a larger monitor, which requires a desk – and some might want several screens. Scientists, politicians, academics and teachers may have an office elsewhere in which they do the bulk of their work, but in common with writers and journalists they still need a workspace which does not have to be packed away every time they finish their tasks. One challenge for the designer will be that these clients also generally need shelf space for books, journals, CDs and files, along with mementoes and other paraphernalia.

FIGURE 4.1: Design by Plankbridge Ltd. Dorset, 2018. A flatpack desk may suffice on a tight budget.

People working from home in the creative industries generally need more space – for them tools, materials, pinboards, cupboards, shelves and tables all come in to play. For example, an embroiderer will need good light, space for threads and a safe, clean spot for canvases. An artist, potter or framer might need a sink and running water to hand. A photographer might be able to work from a computer at home, but all their specialised kit also needs safe storage. In this digital age, few photographers will need a darkroom, but the designer may yet have the challenge of fittings one in. Interior designers who are home based may have moved away from the old cliché of working from the dining room table, but even in the internet age space is required for samples, catalogues, presentation boards and the like.

The workspace might also need to include room for homework, study and hobbies. Most of us know a teenager who likes to spread everything out on the bed, but there will be times when a more structured space is needed, along with privacy, quiet (the only noise required by said teenager being the music which blasts through their headphones) and good broadband speeds.

The creative designer should be able to manipulate space in order to fit these needs in, ideally without disrupting the rest of the household, so with the exception of the person sitting at a laptop in the kitchen everyone gets some dedicated space, and the ideal is going to be an area which can be shut off for most of the time.

Having established within the client's initial brief how much space will be needed, the designer moves on to address the client's own style. That usually comes in a discussion about the whole property, but it is possible to encounter a household where one person is happily messy, and another requires a meticulously laid-out desk that will not be disturbed by anyone. When including space for younger members of the family, it is a good idea to let them find their own style and not allow parents or carers to dictate it. That will be appreciated by the child, and it is rewarding to see someone find their design voice for the first time.

As with the rest of the home, one of the first ideas to emerge from general discussion will be whether the overall look should be traditional, contemporary, transitional, eclectic, retro, Scandi or some personal amalgam of the above. That style can be developed by finding a creative hook, which could be something the client already owns, or an image found in a magazine or online which encapsulates their own dream workspace.

Whatever part of the home is being addressed, the budget will play a vital part. If the workspace is part of a much larger project, it is best to present it as part of the whole; however, a feel for the potential cost will always be useful. Someone on a very tight budget might opt for creative use of flatpack furniture, while a client with a much larger budget and a passion for wood might choose a custom-designed study space in polished hardwood built to an exacting specification.

FIGURE 4.2: Interior design by Mary Leslie. London, 2004. Every part of this custom-designed beech and Marmoleum™ desk is designed to suit the client's exact needs.

The final area to explore during the briefing and concept phases will be the finishes. These will be dictated by the purpose, style, space and budget. An open-minded and creative designer should be able to produce designs which enhance the space and fulfil the broad brief within these parameters by using solutions that are practical, good-looking and above all fit for purpose.

When exploring the best place for home working it makes sense to start with the outside. Is there anywhere on the property where the client could create an office – shed, outhouse, space for a studio at the end of the garden? If there is space for a heated studio in the garden it may be the best option, and has the advantage of being a separate lock-and-leave space. As mentioned in case study 4.2, a standalone space for work or hobbies gives the designer and client plenty of options for fitting out and use.

Potters (whether professionals or hobbyists) create a fair amount of dust, and keeping it away from the main house will be appreciated. The challenge here would be providing heat, light and plumbing for the new space, and the designer will need to ensure that it complies with the necessary regulations, including planning permission. Another example would be a client with a lean-to building which would make an ideal artist's studio, but without the necessary door height it might not qualify as a habitable space, which could mean being unable to heat it through the main central heating system, and its use could therefore be restricted. Creating the right door height might be feasible, but is it economically viable?

The traditional shepherd's hut or tiny house can make a pretty and practical addition to the garden, and will have the advantage of being portable if the client moves in the future.

However, if the outdoors does not yield extra space, is it possible to make a link between the house and any outbuildings, or extend and use the side return in a terraced house? In the United Kingdom there are towns full of terraces whose back areas are being extended by filling in the side return, or carving extensions out of back gardens. The result can be a subtle and imaginative solution to fitting a busy household into a cottage-sized space.

However, where the building envelope is tightly contained, the designer will need to explore the interior and carve out a suitable workspace there.

A traditional terraced house often yields a half-landing, which can make a useful office, study or library. This could be very simple, with a desk, chair and masses of bookcases either side of the window. If space and building controls allow, the designer might be able to build a partition and hide away the study. To make it stay hidden a jib door is always a clever solution, but matching existing doors might be more in keeping with the general feel of the house. It is worth playing around with these ideas to see what suits the client best.

If the client wants to use a spare bedroom or living space for the office, can the workspace be tucked away by running sliding doors across one wall and hiding as much as possible behind them? Fitted cupboards can look sexy, and hide the desk, files, stationery and suchlike, while also leaving room for an occasional guest to hang a dress or a jacket. In a limited space it is best to avoid too many doors opening into the room. (Once open, how does the client move around them?) Mirrored doors give a feeling of space, but not everyone wants to wake up and see themselves in the mirror first thing. Pocket doors are a possibility, but they take up a lot of space, hence the preference for sliding doors. Once the workspace has been hidden away the same room could have a day bed, studio bed with truckle underneath, or even a small double. If the bed is in a corner, what about having a padded headboard on two sides to make it more like a daybed? This is a popular idea with younger clients. If there is not enough space for a full run of wardrobes, is it possible to dedicate a small space for the office kit and use the dressing table for work? Whether the designer opts for a work desk hidden from sight, or a dressing table that must multitask, it is still important to provide a comfortable chair – again, also useful for the occasional guest.

FIGURES 4.4A, 4.4B, 4.4C AND 4.4D: Architecture by Matthew Wood. London, 2013. The clients wanted a larger home office than the existing one, close to their established garden, with the added benefit of an indoor/outdoor shower and in harmony with its surroundings. The resulting neat solution embraces the garden, while also offering privacy when in the shower.

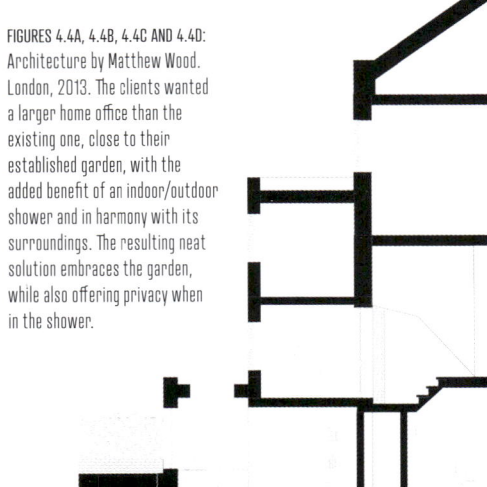

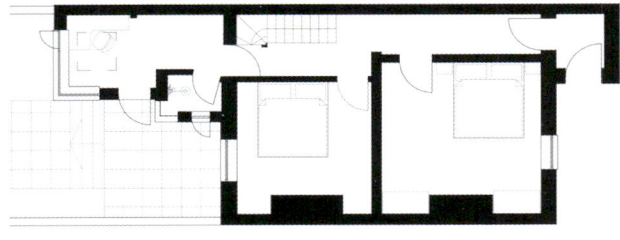

In a living room, similar sliding doors might hide the TV screen, files, and for those who still have them vinyl, CDs and the audio rack. Whichever room the designer uses for a workspace, this is also an opportunity to have a bespoke set of units made. By having the whole bank of cupboards joiner-built, the designer can ensure that it fits the space much better than by using off-the-shelf modules. It may be a simple design built by a local carpenter, or a much more sophisticated set of cupboards designed and built by a specialist joiner. Many bespoke kitchen companies also design and build wardrobes and libraries. It is vital in this case that the designer, either on their own or working with professionals, produces scale drawings for any complex set of units to ensure that they will fit exactly into the space, and to show clearly what can be done with the space on plan, elevation and section.

FIGURE 4.5: Interior design by Mary Leslie. Essex, 2018. Clear, professional plans, elevations and sections are essential for space planning and to help the client understand the concept.

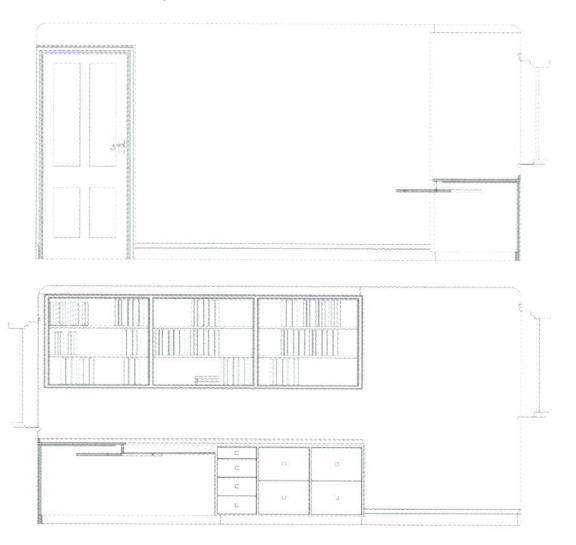

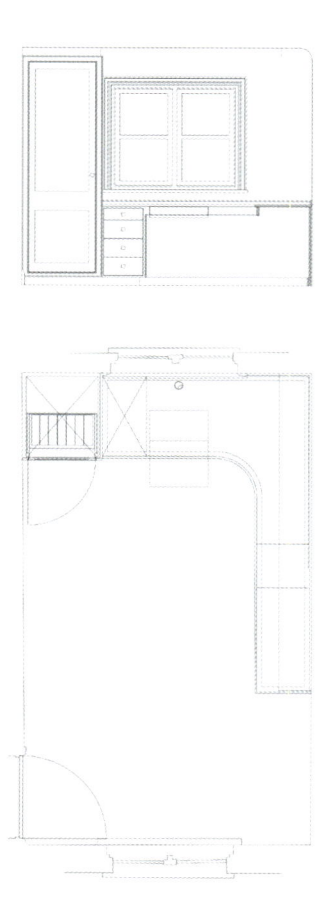

FIGURE 4.6: Architecture by Jarvis Architects, interior design by Mary Leslie. London, 2009. With its window on to the main hall, this bespoke desk enjoys both privacy and natural light for occasional computer use.

It is possible to have a fairly large property where the workspace still has to be squeezed. If it is only needed for occasional work – whether on the computer or for paperwork – it may not be a particularly private space, but borrowing extra internal space can make room for a comfortable and elegant desktop. In a flat there may be places where an internal window can open up a vista from one space to another. It is always preferable to have some natural light, and this is one way of ensuring it.

Space under the staircase is a real multitasker. Not long ago, it was the space best suited to the one and only telephone in the house, and if it has not already been taken over by wine, cleaning materials, WC or coats, perhaps it can return to its roots by accommodating a desktop, shelves, and filing drawers. It might not afford much privacy, but this is a good use of a small, awkwardly shaped yet easily accessible space. The most economical way to create a usable space will be with a piece of kitchen worktop resting on a couple of freestanding filing cabinets. Plain melamine shelves above, cut to shape, will provide space for books. Alternatively, as with the wardrobes or TV room/office, a joinery-built desk, drawers, cupboard and shelves will provide a useful and carefully planned area for desk-based work.

In a small home with children, that dedicated workspace should ideally be in a child-free zone. Sticky fingers, spilt juice and inquisitive, tech-savvy kids are not compatible with the dedicated office laptop. However, the client may want a homework space which is easily supervised, in which case fitting a desk into the kitchen or dining room is worth considering – can it be hidden away? Is there room for pinboards, artwork, files and so on? Somewhere to display the carefully crafted artwork brought home from school is always appreciated. If a space is being created for the children, do the adults need their own workspace too?

If the budget permits, bespoke joinery will always be the best option. The choice of finish, ironmongery, shape and size is so vast that a solution can be found to almost any problem. However, it is wise to persuade the clients to not be too specific. If clients insist on shelves that will fit a particular collection of magazines, added to regularly, ask what will happen if the publisher changes the format. It would be an expensive exercise to alter the bookcases to suit. Other considerations might concern the longevity of the design. All-white might be simple and inexpensive, but will it be durable? Dark colours offset books wonderfully, particularly where there are multicoloured dust jackets, or sets of paperbacks, so painted MDF may be the most cost-effective solution. However, in the truly bespoke the designer has the opportunity to mix endless veneers and to include hidden drawers and cupboards in the room, which can make it so much more special. Add personal touches such as ornaments and photographs, and even a small space will become stylish and inviting.

Architecture by
Wood Architects.
017. A stylish,
chair is always
esk work at home.

Good lighting and comfortable seating have to be top of the list when it comes to the furniture, fittings and equipment. An adjustable desk lamp gives great task lighting, but ambient lighting is also vital. Could you light under the bookshelves? Recessed ceiling lights, wall lights and hanging ceiling lights all have their place in creating ambient lighting. If the client is on a tight budget, clip-on spotlights can be effective, particularly in a retro bedroom for a teenager or student.

Stylists love images of the modern writing table with a few well-chosen accessories and a side chair. The table is fine, but the chair may not be such a good idea. Anyone working for more than half an hour at a time at a desk or table should have a well-designed, ergonomic chair for good support and posture. Too many back problems arise from poor posture at the computer or in the library. It is sound advice to build a fair proportion of the furniture budget into the right chair, with the best ensuring a custom fit for the user including height, rake, seat tilt and arm settings. If the chair may also be used as extra seating, for example in a sitting room, it should still be comfortably upholstered, and it should rotate to make it as versatile as possible.

In the past many people had a writing table or desk for day-to-day running of the home or for personal correspondence. It is still the case that people need room for administration of the household, even if they live in a small flat and their job involves going to an office or another place of work. That admin, such

FIGURE 4.8: Interior design by Mary Leslie. London, 2012. A pretty writing table and some shelves make use of a corner in a small television room.

as banking, correspondence, Christmas cards, present wrapping and similar will require some space, and an elegant writing table or old-fashioned desk should not be dismissed. It can hide the stationery, laptop and all the other paraphernalia. Modern decorative, antique and mid-century modern furniture can all be very useful when it comes to making a small, standalone work area – think kneehole desk, drop-front bureau, bureau bookcase, reclaimed school table or rolltop desk. Well made, well designed and affordable.

The walls, floor, upholstery and desktop or shelf finishes reflect the mood of any space, and the fact that it needs to be practical does not meant it cannot be eye-catching. Tactile surfaces such as leather, rattan, velvet and carriage cloth can make the space warm and inviting. Clever use of mirrors, in a study as much as a bathroom, will create vistas and plays of light that make a room seem larger. One of the most practical surfaces for a desktop is Marmoleum™ rather than leather, as it is easily maintained, durable and good-looking.

With so many areas of the home to choose from, fitting a place to work into the property should be easier than other challenges the designer faces such as an extra bedroom, space to entertain, or storage for the whole family, always a problem in a small home.

Checklist – have you asked the client:

- Do you need one or more workspaces for different members of the household, or can you share?
- Is your workspace primarily for domestic tasks, or will you be using it for your line of business?
- Do you already have a style in mind – is there a look you yearn for but have never had?
- What are your professions/trades/crafts?
- Do you work alone, or do you need room for assistants?
- Will your clients or customers visit you at home?
- For the computer-based, will you have a laptop, desktop or both, and printer, stationery, etc.?
- For the artists and crafters: what equipment will you have – easels, canvases, loom, spinning wheel, lathe, potter's wheel …?
- Do you need plumbing, specialist power, connectivity or light in your workspace?
- What do you already have, and how much do we need to budget for the rest?

FIGURE 4.9: Architecture by Matthew Wood Architects. Greenwich, London, 2019. This writer's room transforms an old garden shed to make a calm, useful and compact space exactly as the client imagined.

DESIGNER	Dean Keyworth of Armstrong Keyworth
CLIENTS	A young Chinese professional couple both occasionally working from home
BRIEF	The couple were unable to have a dedicated home office but requested a room that could be an office, media room and occasional spare bedroom. The husband, who was in charge of approving the room design, requested that it should not be overtly masculine.
LOCATION	Marylebone, Central London
CHALLENGE	The main challenge was to create a room with two distinct uses – sitting room and home office – and the possibility of a third by providing a bed for the occasional guest. It had to be both practical and aesthetically pleasing. The clients were looking for stylish and luxurious finishes which would reflect the high standard of decor in the rest of the flat. They were particularly keen that should the space be used as a media room there would be no sign of the office function.
	The designer created a multipurpose space behind sliding screens with room for a television at high level if required, and office stationery, files and printer easily accessible below. The combination of carefully proportioned sliding lacquered screens allows the clients easy access to their activity of choice.
OUTCOME	In order to avoid an overtly masculine approach to a very linear space, the long wall was traditionally upholstered in an oriental design in silk

FIGURE 4.10: A hand-drawn or CGI visual can help clients imagine the end result.

FIGURE 4.11: The glossy, lacquered screens are both practical and dramatic.

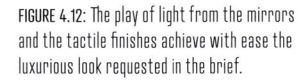

FIGURE 4.12: The play of light from the mirrors and the tactile finishes achieve with ease the luxurious look requested in the brief.

FIGURE 4.13: The choice of fabrics and upholstery are key to completing the look.

stretched over batten and bump. The silk panels also conceal the speakers for the clients' hi-tech sound system.

The glossy red lacquer screens are a nod to the clients' Asian heritage, while also creating a warm ambiance, and the depth of high-gloss colour adds to the luxurious atmosphere of the whole.

Wood veneers were used for the custom-made workspace and display shelves/TV space behind the lacquered sliding doors. Neatly designed drawers hide the stationery, and the simple, retro look of the specialist joinery fits the overall theme.

The floor has been tiled in leather, which is surprisingly durable. The clients and their visitors have been delighted at the way it has matured gracefully, and appreciate how comfortable it is to walk on, while also adding to the acoustic qualities of the room.

The room had very little natural daylight, and clever use of mirrors bounces any light around it. Task lighting enhances the workspace, and downlights show off the clients' collection of art glass – currently displayed in place of a television screen.

For the upholstery the clients opted for linear designs with a more masculine feel; in this case a Dice chair from David Linley and an armchair with coordinating footstool which incorporates a day bed for occasional guests.

The use of luxury materials, flexible space and clever lighting clearly demonstrates the benefits of a truly bespoke interior.

CASE STUDY 4.2: PLANKBRIDGE

DESIGNER   Richard Lee of Plankbridge Ltd, in close collaboration with the client

CLIENT   A keen fisherman

BRIEF   The client had wanted a shepherd's hut for a long time, and when the opportunity arose to create a room for music, reading, fly-tying and as a retreat from work, he decided to grasp it. He and Richard Lee worked closely together to create a fisherman's retreat in a Plankbridge Snug shepherd's hut. Although the client had a broad idea of the look he wanted, it was up to Richard Lee to explain the possibilities and work out how to incorporate them into the limited space.

LOCATION   A North Dorset garden on the bank of a local stream

FIGURE 4.14: A shepherd's hut can squeeze an extra room into the garden.

FIGURE 4.15: The best workspace will reflect the passions of its owner.

CHALLENGE   When designing the interior, the designer had to create zones for fly tying, storage for fishing equipment, a guitar, books, sleeping, reading and heating. The ambiance was to be cosy, welcoming and a retreat from the house, offering a space that the client could return to without having to set up again every time.

The basic design of the Snug hut was very familiar to the Plankbridge team, so the build method was a known quantity that could be varied to suit the client's needs.

To make a workspace, the designer suggested a kneehole desk, which would have drawers of the correct depth to take all the specialist kit for the client's fishing, including his fly-tying equipment, reels, thread, hooks, feathers and so on. Some of the drawers were leather lined to protect fragile items, and the desk has an olive ash top which complements the rustic colours in the hut. The design team provided bookshelves custom made to suit the client's books, as well as larger-format guitar music. The client wisely included a desk chair, which makes sitting for long periods and concentrating on his hobbies more comfortable and better for the posture than an occasional chair.

For heat and light, a 16-amp supply was run ahead of time to the site so that the hut would have ample lighting and some power. A woodburning stove is always a warm and welcoming way to heat a room, and in this case it was easy to incorporate. The alternative would have been an electric cast-iron radiator, which is popular for those wanting something that requires less work to maintain.

The rear of the hut has been designed with a bed, which gives a comfortable spot for reading, resting and the dog. It can also be used as an occasional bed for guests. Small details such as the sheepskin throw, colourful cushions and casual bed linen all make it an inviting corner in which to relax. There is room under the bed platform for more storage, which is always useful. The working shutters give privacy for anyone staying overnight and add character to the room by harking back to shepherd's huts of old.

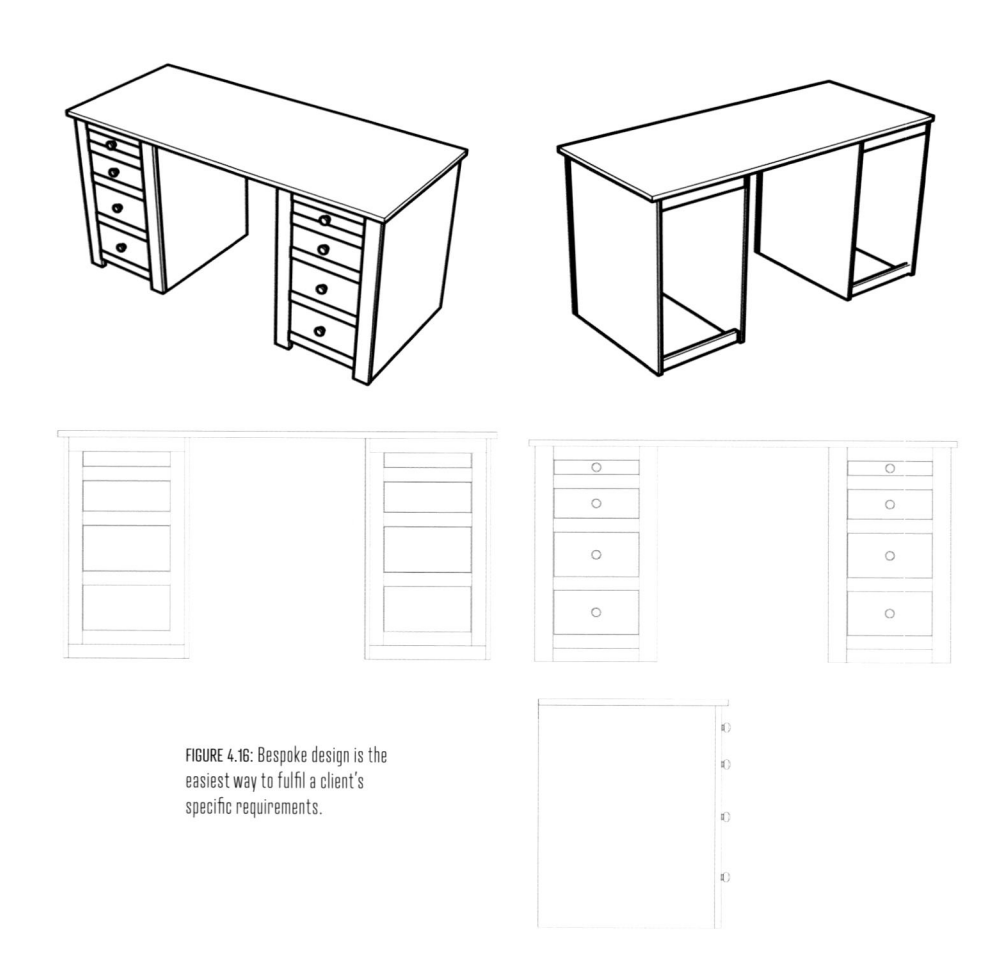

FIGURE 4.16: Bespoke design is the easiest way to fulfil a client's specific requirements.

FIGURE 4.17: A spare bed does not need to be large, just welcoming.

Access to the site was tricky (as is often the case). It was difficult to judge the state of the ground, and although they had hoped to wheel the hut into place, it had to be turned through 90 degrees with a high-lift jack to settle it on site. (Sometimes huts have to be craned into position.) Also, this particular hut did not require planning permission – generally it is not the hut, which is a mobile unit, but its intended use which affects planning permission. Although this hut did not require plumbing, many do, and allowing for a water supply to the hut is another matter for the planning department.

OUTCOME   Once the hut was in place, furnished and ready to use, the client was happy to say it exceeded his expectations; he was pleased he had seized the chance to make it happen.

5

....

THE WET SPACE

....

The client is more likely to have specific ideas about the way they require the wet space to be than almost anywhere else in the house. Whether they have a bath or shower room, they will be particular about the position of everything from the shower hose to the flush button, passing shaving tackle and makeup brushes on the way. To give them a bespoke space the designer will need to talk freely to them about their personal day-to-day habits. However, before delving into the minutiae, the designer must consider the overall look and the potential layout. They will want to balance how the space feels with functionality and the necessary sanitaryware arrangements. Understanding the vision for the whole home will help the designer find a design for the bathrooms which flows naturally from the rest of the space.

It is advisable to spend time thinking about the way the room will feel. Even if it is a small space, is it intended to be cocooning, supremely functional or a traditionally cluttered room which happens to have some plumbing in it? If the ambiance of the whole property is slick and modern, that feel will flow naturally to the finishes and the hardware in the wet space, while clients who like to have furniture, books and plants right through the house will want that to be continued into the bath or shower room design.

The look may evolve as part of the whole, but the layout will largely be governed by the existing plumbing installation in a refurbishment, and the feasible pipe routes in a new build. It is very frustrating for a designer to find that the layout which seemed so perfect in theory is impossible because it would make too many bends in the soil pipe, or because the hot and cold feeds cannot reach the ideal spot for the basin.

In a remodelling project, an extra shower room might be able to use space borrowed from elsewhere. As with any other manipulation of the layout it is important to start with a measured survey showing the existing plumbing installation, particularly the pipe runs and soil stacks. While macerators may seem the answer to putting an extra WC some distance from the existing drainage, even they have their limitations, and it is always wise to

FIGURE 5.1: Interior design by 2LG Studio. Farnham, Surrey, 2018. Traditional and contemporary meld in this neat bathroom enhanced by pretty accessories and carefully tended plants.

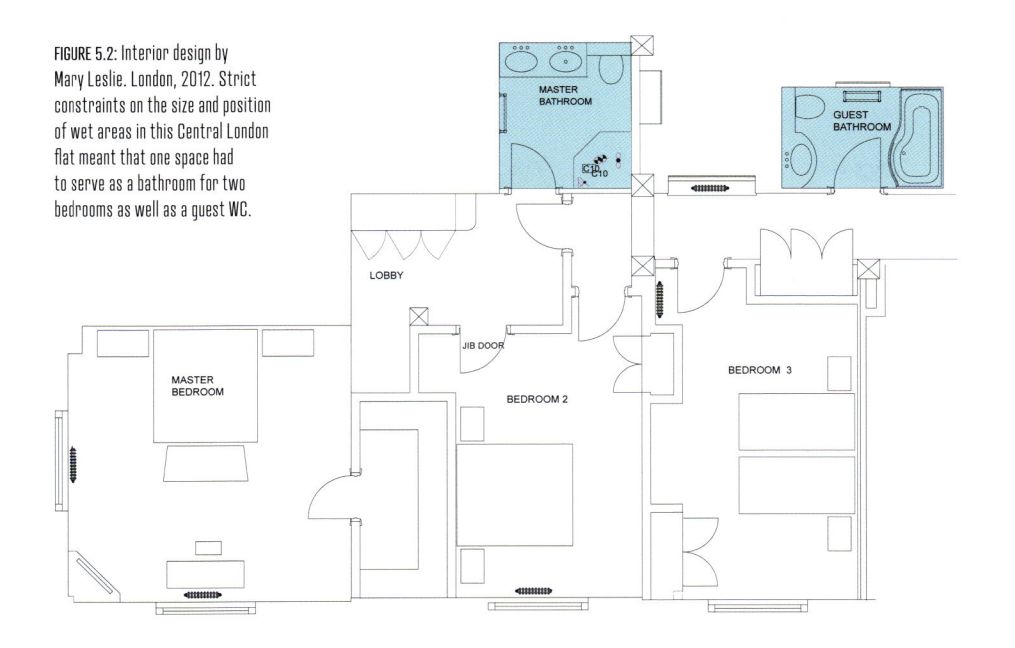

FIGURE 5.2: Interior design by Mary Leslie. London, 2012. Strict constraints on the size and position of wet areas in this Central London flat meant that one space had to serve as a bathroom for two bedrooms as well as a guest WC.

MASTER BATHROOM

GUEST BATHROOM

LOBBY

JIB DOOR

MASTER BEDROOM

BEDROOM 2

BEDROOM 3

check that the proposed layouts are feasible before presenting them to the client. Using a specialist bathroom designer can simplify the process, as they will recognise both the possibilities and the pitfalls of a scheme immediately. Otherwise, it is vital to talk to the contractors from early in the process, as the M&E (mechanical & electrical) engineer or plumber should be able to provide the answers. A designer remodelling a mansion flat or condominium will need to have the relevant licences from the tenants' association or management company. These can be hard to acquire, and it can be frustrating for both client and designer if they are not permitted to increase the footprint of the wet space within a large apartment to accommodate modern requirements. Clients will expect a period property which had two bathrooms and one separate WC for four or five bedrooms when it was built to have at least four if not six nowadays.

Once the designer has a high-level idea of the look and functionality of the space they will need to start discussing the particulars, and for this a detailed questionnaire will be an invaluable tool. Clients often find it easier to describe what they do not want than what they do, and by the end of the process there will be few secrets about their daily routines. The designer will need to handle these questions sensitively and with humour, and be able to gauge whether they are too intrusive, or whether asking the questions will actually help the clients relax and enjoy creating their ideal bathroom. There may be some clients who will answer a handful of questions about the shower and the WC and expect the designer to come up with various proposals, but more engaged clients will appreciate being consulted over the fine details.

FIGURES 5.3A AND 5.3B: Interior design by Field Day Studio. Fulham, London, 2016. One house, two styles. If one occupant asks for modern and the other for traditional there is no reason not to follow the brief, as in this small terraced house.

It will be a much quicker and easier task to visit a bathroom showroom in person or virtually, with or without the clients, if the majority of these questions have been resolved in advance and the designer has a good idea of the way to fit everything into the space. The list of questions will depend on whether the space is a master bathroom, family bathroom or guest bathroom. In a large house where there are several bathrooms – ranging from the large and luxurious to the guest en-suite squeezed into a corner – the principles may remain the same, but the designer needs to think how to adapt them for each specific space.

The questionnaire might include:

1. The client's routine:
- Do you dress and undress in the bathroom or bedroom?
- Similarly, where do you dry yourself?
- Where do you put dirty laundry?
- How many towels do you like to have in your own bathroom?
- Do you use an electric razor/toothbrush? How many sockets will you require, and where do you like to have them in relation to the basin?
- Do you prefer to do your makeup or grooming in the bathroom or bedroom?
- Do you arrange your toiletries and cosmetics in a particular way?
- How close to the mirror do you need to be to see easily when applying makeup?
- Do you need a medicine cabinet in the bathroom?
- Do you like to read in the bathroom?
- Will you need a TV or sound system in the room?

2. The sanitaryware:

- Which would you prefer: a close-coupled or back-to-wall WC or shower-toilet?
- If there is space, would you like a separate bidet?
- Do you have a particular position you prefer for the WC flush plate or handle?
- Would you like the hand basin to be wall mounted, under mounted, vessel or pedestal?
- Do you prefer a mixer tap or separate taps, and what kind of waste would you prefer to use: pop-up, plug and chain, swivel?
- What finish do you want for the hardware? Chrome, nickel, gold-plated, bronze, black chrome or a mixture?
- Would you rather have a walk-in shower, enclosed shower or wet room?
- How do you like to arrange the shower heads and the valves?
- Do you have a preference for rain shower, steam shower, handheld, rain bars or slide bar, and would you like the overall look to be minimalist, contemporary or traditional?
- Do you prefer niches or baskets for toiletries in the shower?
- Do you like to have a toe shelf or a seat at low level?

Armed with all this information, the designer must now think how to be clever and fit all of this in while also making it look interesting. They should remember to ask the client if they already have anything they would like to include in the bathroom, such as furniture, pictures and ornaments.

The designer may find that a client who has firm ideas on the position of the shower hose might not be so sure about the colour scheme or the finishes available. While the client may know that they want to have a very plain, Zen-like space, or a jumble of colour and activity, it is the designer's brief to use their ingenuity and provide the solution.

FIGURES 5.4A AND 5.4B: Wet-room architecture by Izat Arundell. Edinburgh, 2017. Bathroom interior design by Spencer & Wedekind. Wendell Park, London. 2017. Calm or colourful? This simple wet room and funky bathroom show how a creative designer can produce a room to suit either brief.

Once the position of the sanitaryware and the pipework has been agreed, the designer should check whether the client wants every vertical surface and the floor to be a hard finish, such as porcelain tiles, marble, quartz or mosaic. A client with a larger budget might like unusual book-matched marble on the walls and floor, while on a tighter budget oblong brick-bond plain white tiles can be very smart. In a small space, using tiles on every surface can make it feel even smaller, unless something eye-catching is used. Using iridescent mosaics or brightly coloured hand-made Zellige tiles in a very small space, particularly if several colours are in play, is more interesting than having the space clad from floor to ceiling in large, neutral tiles.

To make the space feel less like a compact box it helps to vary the surface finishes, and only tile the walls which will get wet. Clearly in a wet room that will be everywhere, but otherwise having a finish such as panelling, paint or wallpaper will be more interesting and will also allow for a much greater variety of colours and finishes. If the clients are interested in organic forms and amazing colours it is worth suggesting tadelakt, which is like modelling clay, and can be used to create wonderful curves and angles, or polished concrete, which looks harder but is very versatile.

A bathroom can easily be panelled, which is a good way of concealing cupboards or doors, and in a traditional space the use of bead-and-butt boarding or Shaker panels will give a casual, practical effect. While much broken-colour work is out of fashion, there is still a place for a special paint finish on the walls, and lacquer can be wonderful to give a real depth of colour.

FIGURES 5.5A AND 5.5B: Blue WC interior design by Studio Duggan. London, 2017. Terracotta shower by Tadelakt London Ltd. London, 2017. Finishes such as Moroccan Zellige tiles and tadelakt plaster will add colour and drama to a small space.

FIGURE 5.6: Interior design by Mairi Helena. Edinburgh, 2016. Hand-painted walls combined with bright Moroccan tiles enliven an attic shower room.

103

CHAPTER 5   THE WET SPACE

The designer should be careful when suggesting dark colours for the walls, as they require more coats than the average painter or decorator will allow when pricing. Painters and decorators habitually estimate for two or three coats. It pays to be specific about the need for three or even four coats when writing the specification.

In a compact wet space, there will not be much usable floor area, but it can counterbalance the wall finish to create an illusion of space. It is always a good idea in a small home to avoid too many changes of floor finish, so if elsewhere is wood, tile or marble it may be possible to carry this into the wet space. Otherwise, plain walls can be complemented by patterned tiles, or vice versa – but not both patterned, which may confuse the eye. It is rare these days to have a carpeted bathroom floor; however, there may still be clients who request that the carpet run through from the bedroom, in which case best-quality wool/nylon carpet should be used. If the designer has specified underfloor heating with carpet, it is important to ensure that the tog value of the carpet is correct for the floor.

Most clients at the upper end of the market will expect underfloor heating, but it need not be too expensive if the budget is tight. Underfloor heating frees up wall space, and is comfortable to walk on, but the client will need to appreciate that it is not responsive. Where clients only have the central heating on for part of the day, they may want the underfloor heating to be on a separate circuit. The same applies to the towel warmers. If run off the heating, they will only dry towels when the heating is on, whereas if they are run from the hot water, they will warm towels all year round. It is also a good idea to suggest de-mister pads behind the mirrors, which are a thoughtful and functional addition to the room.

One of the best ways of creating the illusion of space in a small room is to have plenty of reflective surfaces, but not every surface should be glossy; it is important to

FIGURES 5.7A AND FIGURE 5.7B: Interior design by Guy Goodfellow. London, 2004. The lacquered bookshelves and cabinets combined with low-level mirror and unusual green/gilt wallpaper all combine to make a well thought-out, unusual guest bathroom.

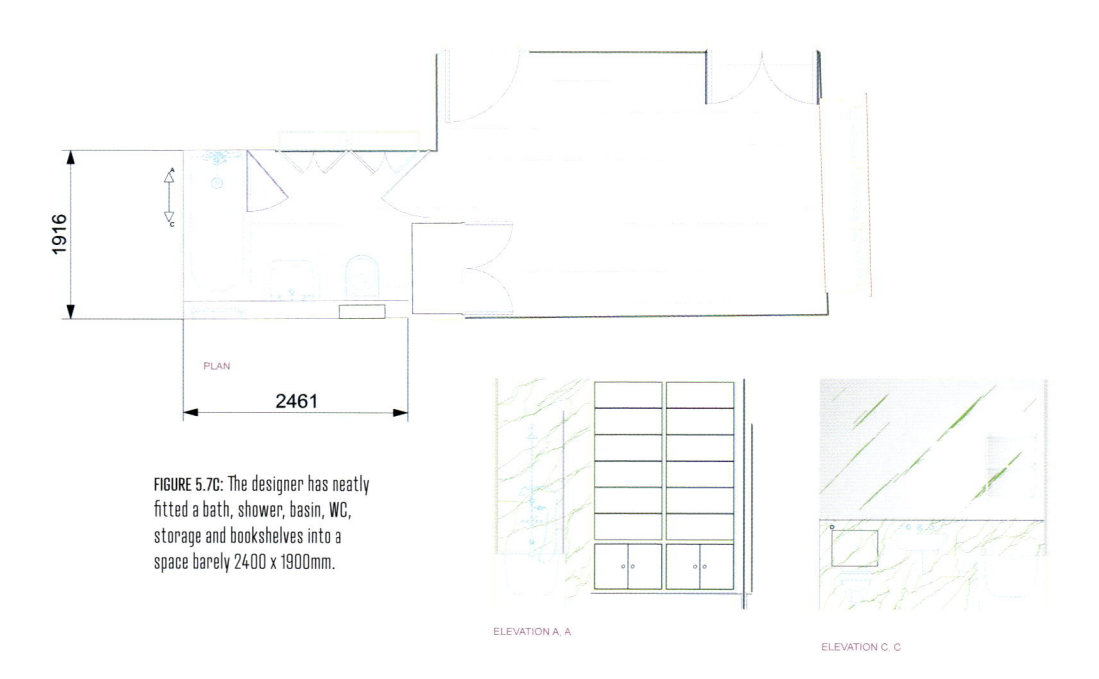

1916

PLAN

2461

FIGURE 5.7C: The designer has neatly fitted a bath, shower, basin, WC, storage and bookshelves into a space barely 2400 x 1900mm.

ELEVATION A, A

ELEVATION C, C

allow for changes in texture as well. A clever idea is to use mirrors, gilt and lacquer to bounce light around the space and to vary the gloss levels and the textures, as in any other room. Even in a small space, the designer can create a sense of drama as well as practicality around the basin, by having shelves, cupboards, a decorative mirror and great lighting. Mirrors can also be used at low level to create an illusion of space by opening up a vista back into the adjoining room.

Many clients like to have the WC tucked away, but it may not be possible to put the WC behind a partition in a compact space, and some clients might prefer to have it beside the bath/shower as the most convenient position. It is never a good look to have the WC opposite the door, and where possible it should be out of sight when the door is open. If it has a concealed cistern, the shelf above can be part of an alcove which provides space for books and ornaments or is turned into a cabinet.

In an old property there may be room for a cupboard or cabinet in the partition walls, so the designer should check the thickness of the walls. A cupboard can be hidden behind a mirror or within panelling. In a very tight space, there may not be room for a wall-mounted cabinet that protrudes over the basin.

An important element of the design will be the hardware. The designer can lead clients away from the obvious chrome if the whole vision warrants it. There is a plethora of amazing colours and finishes available to add interest to the space, such as rose gold, hammered bronze or matt black. The question will be whether the clients prefer uniformity or like the idea of mixing and matching the finishes. Finishes such as hammered bronze or pewter can add textural contrast, while industrial interiors may benefit from blackened metals mixed with chrome. It is, however, wise to specify all of one finish, such as nickel, from one supplier, so that there will not be a variation in colour within that one finish. It is important to ensure that the inner door handle suits the finishes in the wet space too, even if the door furniture for the rest of the property is different.

FIGURE 5.8: Interior design by Mary Leslie. Oxfordshire, 2009. Old houses often have quirky spaces in the walls. Here the gap was used to create a cabinet behind an old gilt-framed mirror.

FIGURES 5.9A AND FIGURE 5.9B: Interior design by Studio Ett Hem. Paris. Subtle lighting and a creative combination of materials make best use of the space in this awkward Parisian attic.

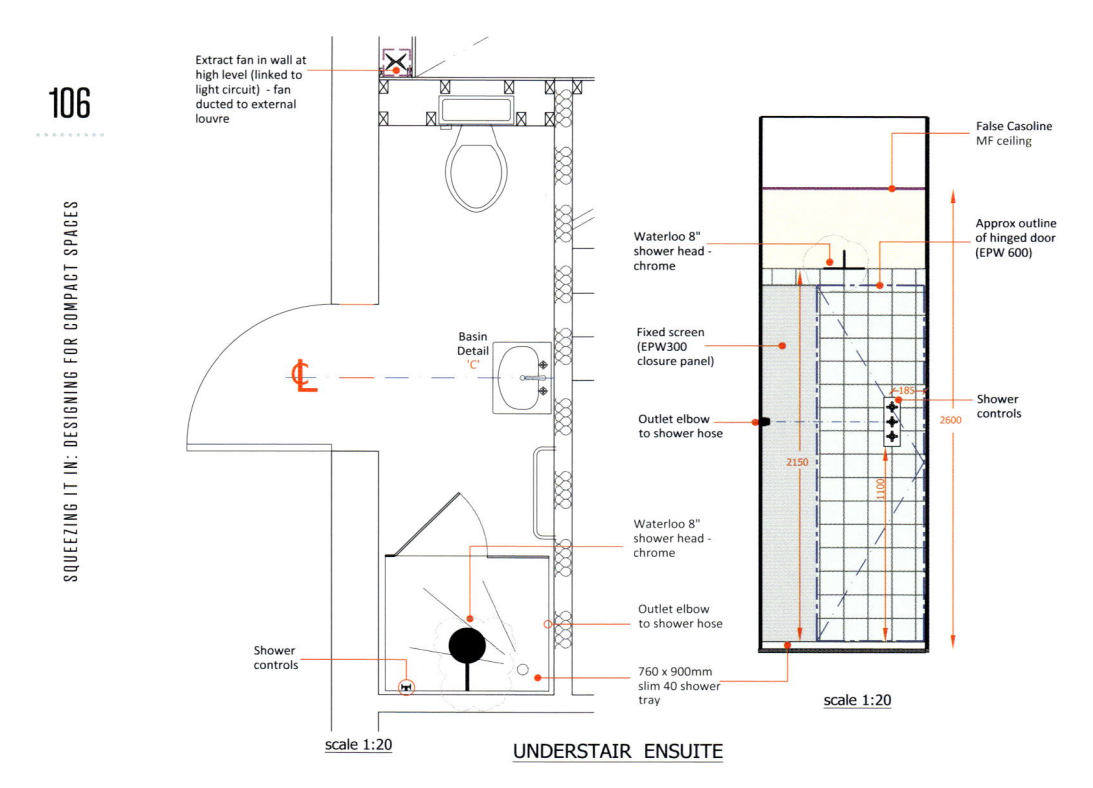

Extract fan in wall at high level (linked to light circuit) - fan ducted to external louvre

Basin Detail 'C'

Shower controls

Waterloo 8" shower head - chrome

Fixed screen (EPW300 closure panel)

Outlet elbow to shower hose

Waterloo 8" shower head - chrome

Outlet elbow to shower hose

760 x 900mm slim 40 shower tray

False Casoline MF ceiling

Approx outline of hinged door (EPW 600)

Shower controls

2600

2150

1100

scale 1:20

scale 1:20

UNDERSTAIR ENSUITE

FIGURE 5.10: Interior design by Mary Leslie and David Morris. Northumberland, 2019. By opening up an unexpected void the designers were able to squeeze an en-suite guest shower room under the attic stairs. Everything had to be fitted in, including shower, basin, WC, ample towels and the visitors' accessories. The designers managed to fit shelves under the turn of the stairs behind the WC, and a towel warmer between the basin and shower.

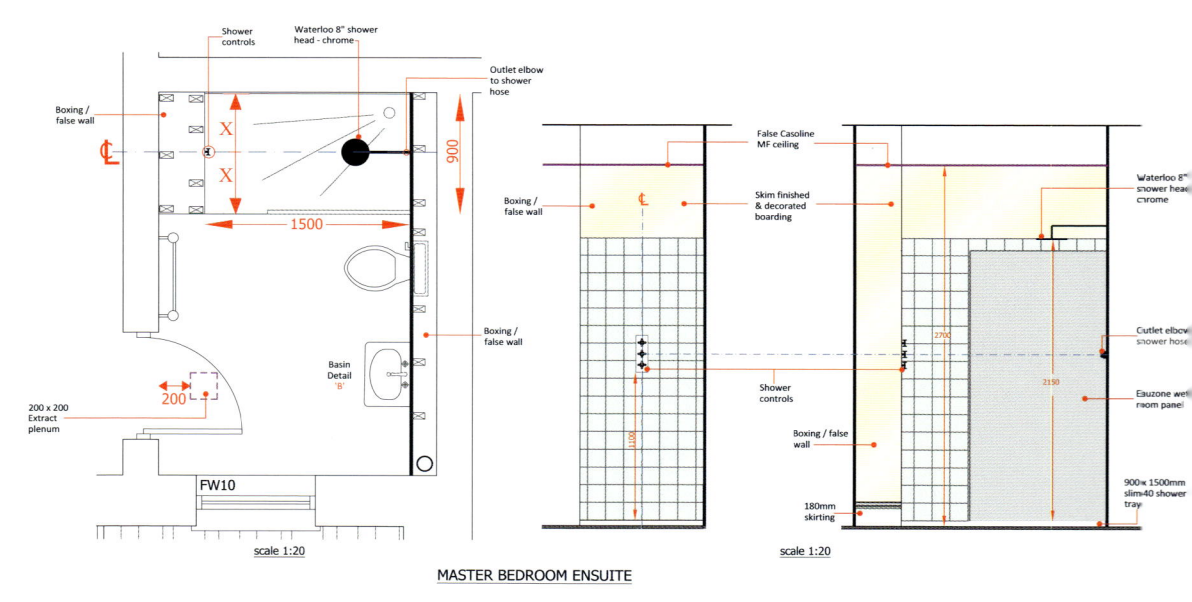

Shower controls

Waterloo 8" shower head - chrome

Outlet elbow to shower hose

Boxing / false wall

900

1500

X X

Boxing / false wall

Basin Detail 'B'

Boxing / false wall

200 x 200 Extract plenum

200

FW10

False Casoline MF ceiling

Skim finished & decorated boarding

Boxing / false wall

Shower controls

Boxing / false wall

180mm skirting

Waterloo 8" shower head - chrome

Outlet elbow shower hose

Eauzone wet room panel

900x 1500mm slim40 shower tray

2700

2150

1100

scale 1:20

scale 1:20

MASTER BEDROOM ENSUITE

FIGURE 5.11: Interior design by Mary Leslie and David Morris. Northumberland, 2019. By building out one end of the shower enclosure and boxing in pipework behind the WC and basin, the designers can ensure that users will not scald themselves on the towel warmer when entering the shower, and will have plenty of room to use the basin and WC. Attention to detail is key to making the space work.

The designer must work out how best to layer the light so that it can be bright for shaving and makeup, dim when visiting at night, and relaxing while having a shower or bath depending on the client's routine. That can all be achieved with a combination of flush-fitted ceiling lights, pendants, low-level LED strips and decorative fittings on either side of the mirror. The mirror lights do not have to be wall-mounted – a pair of lights hanging from the ceiling can also be effective. To achieve the various layers and moods it is essential to use a dimmer, and as with the rest of the property the sophistication of the lighting system will depend on the budget for the project. The position of the switches and the type of lighting in any wet space will also be governed by the local building regulations for electrical fittings.

The designer will often find that clients hope to squeeze in an en-suite shower room for a guest bedroom. This may be carved out of another room or even under a staircase. While shower and WC need to be full-size, the basin can be as narrow as possible, or even set back into the partition. This is a space where the designer can have fun with colour and finish to make a space full of character. Here it might be an idea to have the same effect on the walls and floor, so that the confined space feels like a cocoon.

A master bathroom is very different from a guest bathroom, and the designer will need to consider the needs of the guests. A comfortable guest bathroom will have space for a sponge bag and any basic necessities a visitor might forget. It is always frustrating to stay in a place where there is no room to unpack makeup or hang a toiletry bag on arrival.

Children's spaces can be fun, and colour or movement will make them more engaging. They are more likely to need a bath than a shower, but it does not have to be full-length. As many hooks, shelves and pictures as can be fitted in, or an amusing mural or wallpaper, will turn bathtime into playtime in even the smallest of bathrooms.

While the client might have a firm view of the way they want their own space to be, they will often have less of an idea for a small WC or cloakroom. This is therefore a place to do something crazy or indulgent. Mad wallpaper, a mural, fantastic tiles

FIGURE 5.12: Interior design by Lifedesign. London, 2019. A baby bath is ideal for small children in this colourful children's bathroom.

and lots of reflective surfaces can all be used. Using lights and a decorative mirror with an interesting shape gives character; having one whole wall mirrored is also a good trick, as it reflects the wall finish in the rest of the space. If the WC has a concealed cistern the space above is ideal for shelves or a cupboard, and below can be designed to conceal the toilet rolls and other paraphernalia. Paperback books do not take up much space, and creating a libraloo is a fun way to display books. Even the smallest WC can also be used to hang a collection of photos or prints, and washing the walls with light or having a backlit ceiling can add a touch of glamour to the space. Using an unusual surround for the basin is also a good way to give the room personality. The designer might repurpose an old chest of drawers and add a marble top with an inset or vessel basin, or find a wonderful piece of waney-edged wood or marble to use as a vanity top. All of these can make a space so much more fun.

It may not be possible to avoid the WC being opposite the door from the hall – but if the hall is panelled or has an interesting wall finish, the designer can conceal the room completely by specifying a jib door clad in the same finish as the hall, so that the WC becomes a secret space.

The soft furnishings, furniture and fittings can also be used to give character to a confined wet space. Roman and roller blinds at the window will soften it as well as giving privacy. Old-fashioned net curtains may be out of vogue, but lace panels can be pretty and appropriate at a large enough window. The client may have

CLOCKWISE FROM LEFT

FIGURES 5.13A: Darren Oldfield, London, 2019. **5.13B:** Ben Tindall Architects, Blue Cabin by the Sea, Scotland, 2012. **5.13C:** Mary Leslie, London, 2003. **5.13D:** 2LG, Studio Forest Hill, London, 2016. Strong colours, wallpaper, mirrors, art and books can all add character to cloakrooms and WCs.

FIGURE 5.14: Interior design by Jeffreys Interiors. Perthshire, Scotland, 2012. Specialist joinery makes good use of the space, and a subtle wallpaper enhances a Scottish country bathroom.

furniture or artwork which they want to include in the scheme, and it is vital in every area of the home to give them the opportunity to use or create collections that are personal to them. When working out the budget it is important to leave sufficient for the 'bathroom smalls' – towel rails and rings for hand towels, robe hooks, toilet roll holders and stands, shower baskets. All of these can be both practical and decorative, but to supply them for several bath and shower rooms adds considerably to the overall cost.

The designer should not be surprised by the amount that can be squeezed into a small space. Their art lies in creating a space which the user will appreciate, even luxuriate in, without the benefit of big windows, high ceilings or a large budget.

Checklist – have you asked the client:

- What are your morning and evening routines?
- Do you prefer a bath, shower or both (assuming you can fit them in)?
- Who will be using the bath/shower room?
- Is the room for daily or occasional use?
- Given the feel of the rest of the property, do you have a style in mind such as minimalist, colourful, eclectic or traditional?
- What type and colour of sanitaryware would you like?
- Do you have any preferences for the hard surfaces on walls and floor such as tiling, marble, wood, panelling or glass?
- What storage will you need?
- What electrics would you like, for example shaver socket, hard-wired TV, sound system, heated mirror, towel warmer, and overhead, wall-mounted and low-level lighting?
- Which would you prefer for the window treatments — frosted glass, blinds, curtains or shutters?
- Is there anything you dream of having in this space which you have not been able to have elsewhere?

CASE STUDY 5.1: DARREN OLDFIELD ARCHITECTS/ IMPERFECT INTERIORS

DESIGNER Darren Oldfield Architects and Beth Dadswell of Imperfect Interiors collaborated on the project.

CLIENTS A couple approaching retirement who wanted a pied-à-terre in Central London with space for themselves and a small guest bedroom

BRIEF The brief for the architects came by virtue of the constraints within the property. The flat had a scrappy, old-fashioned layout which needed to be completely reworked in order to contain an open-plan living room, two bedrooms, a shower room, laundry cupboard and two WCs. The architect would need to handle the listed building consents and incorporate the M&E as unobtrusively as possible. For the interior designer the brief was to create a bright and airy feel with simple, mid-century furniture and tactile highlights, and for everything to be easily maintained.

LOCATION A small upper-floor flat in a listed building in London's Notting Hill

CHALLENGE The clients changed design team partway through the project, and the architect took great care to listen to their concerns and needs before working out how to proceed. The listed building consent was a major consideration, and care had to be taken that the new plumbing, specialist joinery and fittings would not damage the structure of the building. The biggest challenge was incorporating the services to make the new layout functional. Three macerators had to be included, which led back to the original soil and vent pipes, along with a central extraction system ducted to the atmosphere. In order to present their case to the authorities the architect demonstrated by a series of drawings and models how the ducting could be concealed within the envelope.

The clients were overseas for much of the project, and ensuring that they understood the limitations imposed by the listed building status, and the procedure in the United Kingdom for undertaking the work, was a challenge itself. Many overseas clients will be familiar with the process in their own

FIGURE 5.15: This deceptively simple shower room belies the effort that went into its design.

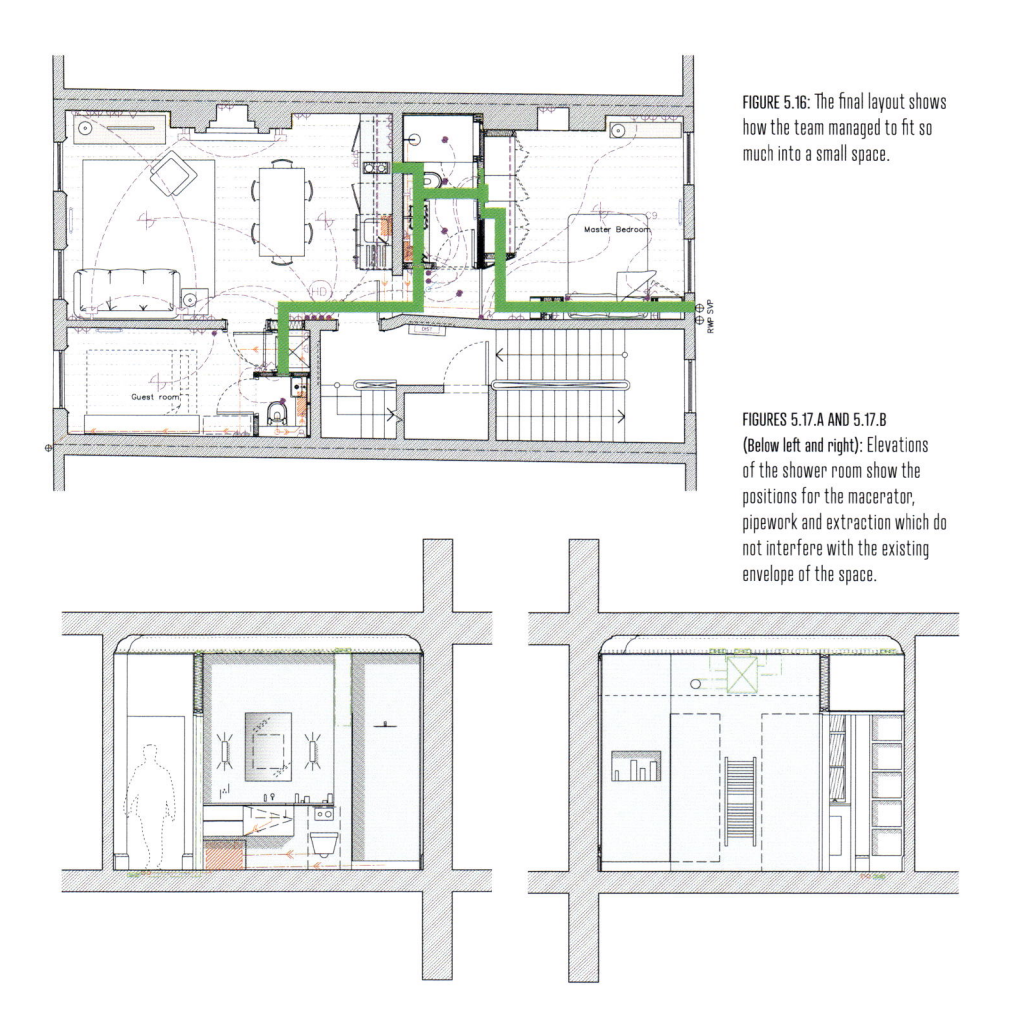

FIGURE 5.16: The final layout shows how the team managed to fit so much into a small space.

FIGURES 5.17.A AND 5.17.B (Below left and right): Elevations of the shower room show the positions for the macerator, pipework and extraction which do not interfere with the existing envelope of the space.

country, but will not necessarily appreciate that this does not translate to another jurisdiction. As the clients were in California for much of the project communication was key, and plenty of drawings, sketches and other details explained the process in detail. Once the clients understood the implications of the plan, they were happy to proceed, and glad to restore the Georgian details to their former elegance.

The architect and designer worked through a series of possible layouts before agreeing on the final design, which squeezed a lot into a small space. They collaborated on internal joinery designs, and electrical circuits and layouts, and while the architect worked on the considerable technical elements of the M&E the designer was able to concentrate on the fixtures, furniture and equipment (FF&E). The clients specifically requested that they would be able to see through from the front to the rear of the flat, and the design team cleverly positioned the main wet space in the core so that this could be achieved.

FIGURE 5.19: The boiler has been concealed in a bedroom cupboard without interfering with the comfort of the clients.

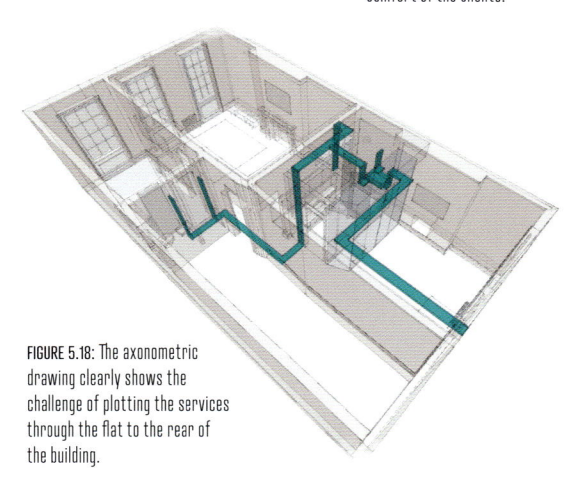

FIGURE 5.18: The axonometric drawing clearly shows the challenge of plotting the services through the flat to the rear of the building.

FIGURE 5.20: Much skill went into concealing the M&E, to create a calm and elegant space from such a challenging brief.

The clients naturally gravitated towards very neutral, pale colours. The designer encouraged them to use bold black fittings to create some contrast, and textured finishes such as the polished plaster in the shower room and leather accents in the living room provide further interest and accents.

The wet spaces were contained in two areas, with the shower room squeezed into the middle of the flat between the kitchen and main bedroom. All the services had to be located both for that space and for the small guest WC and laundry cupboard, so they would not interfere with any of the original detailing that the conservation officer sought to preserve. The solution was to conceal them in dropped ceilings, stud partitions and under the floor. Even a small flat needs plant and machinery to function, and looking around the finished apartment it is hard to see where it is, including the boiler hidden in a false wardrobe in the bedroom, and the macerators in the vanity unit in the shower room.

OUTCOME

The clients were delighted with the transformation, and use the flat as a base to explore Europe when they visit. The design team were able to make a small flat feel spacious and uncluttered, yet comfortable enough for the clients to enjoy with friends.

DESIGNER   Kumiko Ishiguro of Atelier Favori

CLIENTS   There were three different clients with varying budgets and available space. First, a professional client with a custom-designed apartment in Tokyo looking for a high-end finish; second, a young family with limited space who knew they would have to compromise; third, a client with a rental property being renovated at low cost.

BRIEF   The principle behind all three bathroom designs was the same. The preference was for a wet-room shower next to the bath so that the occupant could wash before stepping into the bath. All three spaces had to be easy to maintain, fully tanked and make the best use of the space.

LOCATION   All three apartments are in Tokyo, Japan

FIGURE 5.21: The ideal bathroom has a separate shower close to the bath.

FIGURE 5.22: The clean lines, strong lighting and useful storage space ensure that the bathroom will be a practical space for all the family.

CHALLENGE The main challenge for the designer in all three cases was lack of space. Where possible the shower should be separate from but close to the bath. A non-slip floor, warm to the touch, efficient tanking and adequate drainage were all essential. The contractors were accustomed to these types of installation; the finish is generally driven by cost.

In the high-end bathroom the selection of fittings including tiles, bottle racks, grab-handle shower hose and controls were all carefully coordinated and placed to the client's exact requirements. The bathroom was fully tanked for efficiency. Where there is space for a separate shower the family may bathe one after the other, using the shower to wash but sharing the bath water later on. Out of shot in Figure 5.21 is an enclosed flatscreen television so that the client can watch television from the bath.

The second bathroom was a very confined space, and it was necessary to combine bath and shower, so a modular enclosure was used. Modular systems with enclosed cubicles are a typical way of keeping costs down,

FIGURE 5.23: The custom-made modular system provided an enclosed bath and shower, leaving plenty of room for the WC, basin and storage in a long narrow bathroom.

FIGURE 5.24: A white modular unit and high-level towel rack add much-needed storage space for the family. With no natural light, strong wall and ceiling lighting was essential.

as was the case for this client. The module is made from moulded plastic, with a large pan underneath to avoid any leakage. Typically, clients can choose from a wide range of colours and shapes; however, in this instance the client remained with white, and a custom-made enclosure running across the width of the room made the best use of the space.

The shower-toilet combines WC and bidet in one hygienic item of sanitaryware. Being rimless, it harbours fewer germs than a conventional Western WC, and it was the clear choice for the room. A traditional pedestal basin with single mixer tap made the room feel less angular, and the client preferred this over more modular furniture. Fortunately, as the room was long and narrow there was space for a full-height storage unit by the narrow bathroom door to contain toiletries and other items.

By contrast, the rental bathroom had to contain a separate bath and shower in a confined space on a very tight budget. In this instance there are few fittings for the shower other than the flexible hose, so that the head can be used in both bath and shower. Lighting is from a simple wall light, and in place of a glazed enclosure there is a shower rail and curtain. However, the principle of showering before bathing endured even in such a small space and at a lost cost.

OUTCOME All three clients were pleased with the results, which came within their budgets. While a custom bathroom costs much more than the system version, the modules were easy to maintain and functional. By using a custom-designed modular bathroom for the combined bath and shower the designer was able to make the best of both high and system detailing, such as the choice of tiles and inclusion of pretty niches for bottles and accessories to give the room a character of its own.

FIGURE 5.25: The fittings for the rental bathroom are all as simple and economical as possible, while still enabling the tenant to shower and bathe separately.

FIGURE 5.26: An asymmetric arrangement of niches adds character to the modular bath and shower enclosure.

CASE STUDY 5.3: MATTHEW WOOD ARCHITECTS

FIGURE 5.27: Renovation of this derelict wash house to make a studio and shower room was a challenge to relish.

DESIGNER : Matthew Wood Architects

CLIENT : An author looking for a retreat at the bottom of the garden complete with en-suite shower room

BRIEF : The project involved taking a ramshackle, derelict wash house at the end of the client's sloping London garden and turning it into a haven with a studio/writing room and en-suite shower room. The revitalised shed would also tie the two ends of the garden together, with the upper level relating to the house and the lower level to the writing room. Each terrace was to be designed to catch the sun at a particular time of day. The finishes were to be kept simple and the project needed to be completed on a tight budget.

LOCATION : Greenwich, London

FIGURE 5.28: The two new terraces link the house, garden and new studio space much more effectively than the old, sloping lawn.

FIGURE 5.29: The site plan shows how small the overall footprint is, and how tight the space was for the new shower room.

FIGURE 5.30: A full set of elevations demonstrates how carefully each item had to be placed to fit into the space.

CHALLENGE

The architect wanted to avoid demolishing the shed completely, and to reflect its origins. He had to use a new steel-framed building and replacement slab to tie in the existing retaining walls and shore up the slope, which would allow the garden to be terraced. The client took the opportunity to improve the upper level by matching the doors at the rear of the house on the upper level with the new ones in the writing room.

He was keen to recycle where possible, and specified that the studio and shower room should be built partly with bricks from the old wash house and partly with Crittall-style doors and windows. The flat roof would be laid with sedum to reflect the overgrown roof of the original.

Happily, the client had a boat-builder friend who undertook much of the construction. He understood the need to make every millimetre work, particularly where the tiny shower and WC had to share a partition wall with the bookcases for the writing room. Materials such as the birch ply on the writing room side were only 12mm or 8mm thick in places, and the

FIGURE 5.31: The Barbican basin sits neatly within the wall without overly encroaching on valuable space on the studio side.

shelves were designed to fit around an iconic, space-saving Barbican sink (a model now sadly discontinued by the manufacturers), whose upright design meant that it occupied little valuable space in the stud partition separating the two rooms.

Natural light was fed into the shower through high-level clerestory windows to match the new front of the building as well as a glazed door to the writing room, whose clever positioning meant privacy for any occupant of the WC.

The choice of materials such as the birch ply was largely driven by cost, and the plain subway tiles were also an economical and practical finish from floor to ceiling in the shower room – which, like the Crittall-style doors and windows, gave a twentieth-century modern feel to the space.

OUTCOME The client was pleased to have an extra space that could act as a retreat and also be used as a guest bedroom with en-suite shower room when necessary.

FIGURE 5.32: Natural light and plain reflective surfaces ensure a serviceable space in keeping with the aim and budget for the project.

6

THE REST OF IT

It does not matter whether the client has a reasonably sized house, a cottage or a very small flat – there will be spaces which cannot be used for living, sleeping, cooking or eating, yet are essential to the smooth running of the home. If the designer considers basic everyday actions, these will include: using coats and outdoor shoes; storing cleaning materials and the iron/ironing board; laundry, drying and the linen cupboard; space for the Christmas decorations, bottles, sports kit and other items – essentially storage, storage and more storage. The designer will need to use every centimetre of the site wisely to accommodate the client's needs. The areas once referred to as the 'back premises' may consist of a single 600mm-wide cupboard, or a tricky space under the stairs which also houses the hot water tank, meters and fuse board. However, there might be an attic, space on the stairs or an under-street vault, and all can be pressed into service.

Just as when planning a sleeping space to accommodate clothes, or a living space to allow for hobbies, the designer needs to question the client's daily requirements to make sure their designs will make best use of the rest of the home. The remaining nooks and crannies, open spaces and under-used areas must be made to work hard.

FIGURES 6.1A AND 6.1B: Interior design by Darren Oldfield Architects, London. Removing the collection of glass to one landing and a desk to another uses the landings in this loft conversion to free up space in the living area.

Storage is always going to be an issue in a compact space, but thinking creatively about the available space may reveal areas that will take books, suitcases, linen and the rest, while also looking aesthetically pleasing and showing the designer's skill at manipulating space.

The designer might be asked to accommodate large suitcases for overseas travel in a one-bedroom pied-à-terre, or three dinner services in a flat with a small kitchen. Other clients might want to store a collection of fine wines with the necessary temperature controls, or may need a gun cupboard which requires very specific siting. What if the clients collect art glass, or have hundreds of books? If they cannot be displayed in the living room, they may need to be housed on or under the stairs.

Once houses ceased to have a scullery there was a time when the washing machine was either situated in the kitchen, or a trip to the launderette was a weekly necessity. However, nowadays designers are more likely to be asked to create a separate utility space for laundry and cleaning materials even in the smallest of flats. That does not have to be a whole room; it could be a very well-designed cupboard. Clever manipulation of a small space can provide room for a washing machine/ tumble dryer, ironing board and detergent, and perhaps even space to hang clothes.

When a designer starts to work with new clients it is easy to spend so much time on the main rooms that meetings run out of time without considering the rest. It is therefore a good idea to suggest starting a meeting with the minor areas, and taking the client through those before discussing the living/sleeping/cooking/wet spaces. The best way to do this is by walking the client around the house on plan, which means starting at the front or back door and thinking step by step where they will put things.

Come in the door in wet coats – where do they hang them, and is there room for wet hats, boots and shoes too? What about guests' coats? Is there room for a table or shelf to put keys and post on, which is not within reach of the letterbox? (Savvy burglars can get at anything within reach by using a pole and hook poked through it.) Even in a small hall or cloakroom it is a good idea to include a bench or seat so that people can sit down to deal with boots and shoes.

FIGURE 6.2: Interior design by Eva Byrne of Houseology. Dublin, 2019. An amazing amount can be fitted into a small space with careful planning. This neat cupboard in an alcove barely 800mm wide has space for most laundry needs.

FIGURE 6.3: Interior design by Eva Byrne of Houseology. Dublin, 2019. Even a very small hallway can have space for coats, shoes and a key shelf.

FIGURE 6.4: Interior design by Eva Byrne of Houseology. Dublin, 2003. Clean lines and simple storage make this mews house cloakroom seem larger than it is.

It may be that the coats have to hang in the guest WC. The designer should look for ways of making the whole look decorative rather than scruffy. Who wants to get too close to wet coats or old trainers when visiting the loo? Perhaps the designer can make a statement with hats, or incorporate wicker baskets for piles of teenage shoes.

Progressing through the house with the client, the designer should imagine the utility or laundry area. Very probably there is none, but can it be created? Is it just space for a washer/dryer and sink, or does it also need room for cleaning materials, vases, dogs and cats? Can the designer fit narrow shelves above the appliances, or above the cistern in a WC (which is a good place to create a display of vases or jars)? Looking at the property on plan, might it be possible to split a bathroom in half to make a laundry cupboard back-to-back with a shower room?

Some clients might have space for a separate utility room which must serve several purposes. Where this is not needed for other activities, it should be carefully planned and easily maintained. The designer needs to bear in mind that there may be restrictions on the position of the plumbing, particularly in blocks of flats. However, if the client is looking for a separate laundry room, it is worth questioning whether it is really necessary. There are ways of creating a useful utility space without taking up an entire room in the house.

There is often a space at the bottom of a flight of stairs which could easily become a walk-in store, a wine cellar or a laundry. One of the main challenges when looking for space to put a laundry will be plumbing in the sink and washing machine. If the cupboard is back-to-back with a bathroom or WC that should not be a problem. Most architects and designers will agree that pumps should be used as a last resort, so if some form of mechanical draining is necessary it is wise to engage a plumber or M&E engineer early to work out the finer details of pipe runs and falls, before committing to a plan that may prove impossible to implement.

FIGURES 6.5A AND 6.5B: Interior design by Darren Oldfield Architects. London, 2019. The space behind this modern staircase has been well used to provide a utility cupboard, while staying true to the clean, masculine look of the whole.

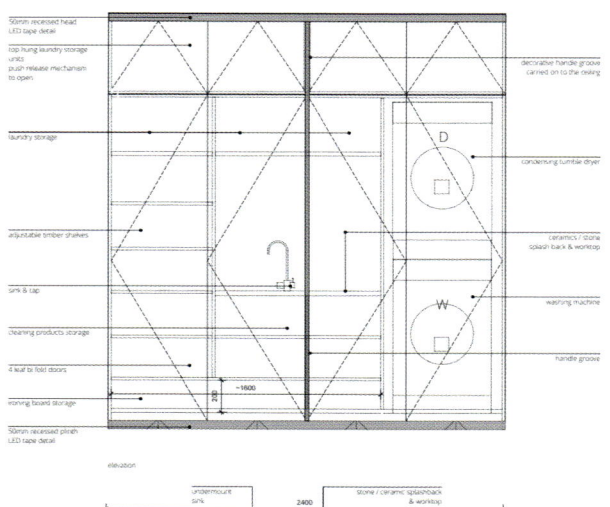

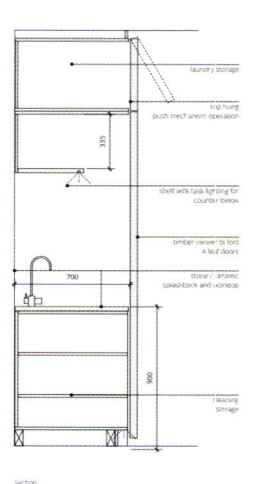

FIGURE 6.5C: Interior design by Darren Oldfield Architects. London, 2019. The construct on drawing shows how the plumbing issues are addressed.

FIGURE 6.6: Interior design by Armstrong Keyworth. London, 2008. Both wine and books are neatly displayed in the lobby of this tiny London flat.

If the space under the stairs has been requisitioned for the laundry, the wine buff may ask for special storage for their wine elsewhere. Many clients living in small homes will only need room for a few bottles of wine, and these can be imaginatively stored around the place.

However, wine storage becomes bulky and technically challenging when the clients stray beyond that rack or small fridge in the kitchen. As the designer walks through the property with the client the information that there are several hundred bottles of vintage wine to be kept on the premises could be daunting; however, there are various areas which can be exploited to solve the problem.

Period townhouses with basements may well have under-street storage, which can be used to squeeze in extra mini rooms. These could become the laundry, a place to store golf clubs or perhaps the bar, but one of best uses of the space will be for wine storage. Clients wanting to keep wine at home may have stringent requirements for temperature

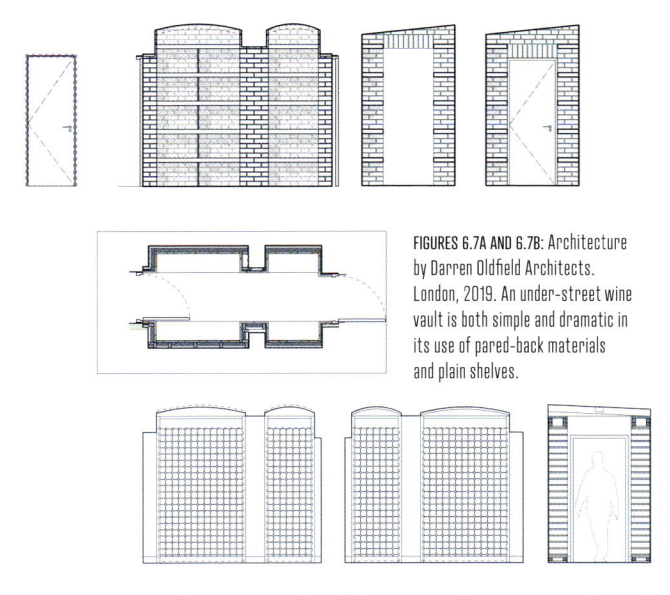

FIGURES 6.7A AND 6.7B: Architecture by Darren Oldfield Architects. London, 2019. An under-street wine vault is both simple and dramatic in its use of pared-back materials and plain shelves.

and humidity control. This is an area where considerable research is required, and in the absence of a knowledgeable architect or surveyor to resolve the technical aspects the designer is advised to involve an expert. Space will be required not just for the wine, but for the air-conditioning unit, flow and return pipework, condenser, power supply and lighting. Some clients will be happy with wine stacked on shelves; others will want space for wooden wine crates, individual wine racks, diagonal bins, a tasting table (a shelf in a small space) and the paraphernalia that goes with storing and tasting fine wine.

While walking around a property on plan there will probably be several proposed uses for the basement or ground-floor understairs space. The designer may want to claim it for the guest WC, coats, laundry or desk, but this too makes an excellent spot for wine storage.

In an entrance hall the wine wall can make a fine talking point and be a useful focus for entertaining in a home where guests flow from the front to the back of the house. Clients might not want to hide a collection of fine wine in a cupboard. However, precision engineering will be required to create a bespoke solution, such as sloping frameless doors with custom patch hinges.

FIGURE 6.8: Interior design by Cellar Maison. Richmond. The understairs space is ideal for displaying a collection of fine wine in this Georgian townhouse.

FIGURE 6.9: Interior design by @homefunkyhome. Wrapping doors and entire walls with shelves is an ideal way to display books and ornaments.

FIGURE 6.10: Architecture by Mary Arnold-Forster Architects. Highlands of Scotland, 2019. The link corridor in this new build house in the Highlands is used to display a book collection toplit by a glass ceiling and unobtrusive wall lights.

The depth of the space should allow plenty of room for the pivot doors, as well as concealing the pipework, cables, climate control unit and double-depth bottle storage.

Even in a compact space there should be room to house books. Clients often believe that books are larger than the reality. Shelves barely 150mm deep can house paperbacks, and the rest may not need more than 250mm. These can be wrapped around doorways, on windowsills and in any other small space not yet taken up by other displays.

In a new build, the architect or designer can take advantage of corridors, links or awkward spaces to create room for cupboards, books and ornaments. Otherwise, dark areas may be lifted by the clever use of skylights or slit windows.

The designer and client have not exhausted all their storage options until they reach the eaves, if they are fortunate enough to have them. Attic or eaves storage is the best place for household detritus such as suitcases, Christmas decorations and the accumulation of family stuff which so many people do not like to throw away. It may not be the sexiest part of the brief but making sure that even these areas are part of the design will make the whole feel finished with care. The designer needs to appreciate that not all their clients will be keen on modern, minimalist living. They also do not need to make every corner into a design statement. If there is a loft it may only need a loft ladder and some hard flooring to make it a useful place for seldom-used items.

The hall, staircase or landings, even when they are small, are great areas for interesting colours and designs. A receptive client might be prepared to have crazy wallpaper or a mural if they do not have pictures. Just as painting a room in a light colour does not necessarily make it lighter, so a dark space can be enhanced by painting it a dramatic colour.

Flooring has to be practical, so most clients will opt for a hard floor around the entrance and anywhere which involves plumbing, mud or dogs. It is sensible to have hard bases to cupboards, which otherwise are inclined to accumulate fluff. However, a staircase is generally better carpeted, which makes it quieter and less slippery. Teenagers thundering up and down a wooden staircase make a lot of noise.

At this point the designer can lead the clients back to the front hall. This is obviously where visitors have their first impression of the property, and even if it is a small space it needs careful thought. It is human nature for visitors to check themselves in a mirror when entering and leaving, so it is useful to hang one near the entrance door.

FIGURE 6.11: Interior design by René Dekker, London, 2016. Dramatic colours and bold artwork link the living room and hall in this Chelsea pied-à-terre. The exceptionally neat pocket doors give an open-plan feel to an otherwise very compact entrance.

FIGURE 6.12: Interior design by 2LG Studio. St Albans. 2018. Even the smallest of entrance halls can be made fun, and can introduce the character of the house within.

FIGURE 6.13: Interior design @wheelspin_chesham. The wall space on a staircase is an ideal spot for creative picture hanging.

The hall, corridors, staircases and landings are also great places to hang pictures of all shapes and sizes. Anything from framed family photographs to assorted landscapes can be creatively arranged to give the space interest. With a bit of quizzing the designer may find that the client already has an interesting collection of mementoes, which can be framed and used to fill gaps. Theatre programmes, album covers, cartoons and old maps can all be used in this way.

While metaphorically walking the client around the house, it remains true to the principle of creating space that the designer should look to the outside as well as the inside for extra space. People living in the countryside might have a more relaxed attitude to putting the deep-freeze or washing machine in an outhouse or the garage to leave more space in a cottage, but in towns they will probably have to stay within the existing envelope. Even a family-sized house can benefit from a utility room added at the back or side. Clever design can make it part of the whole, and it does not have to be large. Knocking a doorway through into a lean-to shed or redundant boiler house can create all the extra space the client needs. Careful thought needs to go into the opening, which seems a minor thing, but involves building regulations and in an old building can be more onerous than the designer intended.

As the designer walks the client around the property on plan, possibilities may arise which were not immediately apparent to the client. The designer should have solutions ready before the client meeting.

Checklist – have you asked the client:

- Can we manipulate the space to create a better layout that will give us the storage we need?
- Is there anywhere else in or around the property that we can use for storage?
- How do you like to store coats, boots and so on?
- Do you have pets, and where do they sleep, live and eat?
- Do you prefer a separate washing machine and tumble dryer, or combined?
- How do you like to keep linen, and how much?
- How many suitcases will you have? Can they be stored under the beds?
- Do you have sports equipment such as golf clubs, skis or racquets which need to be accessible?
- Would you like to display fine wine or other collections?
- How many pictures do you have, and can we hang them in collections around the hall, staircase or landings?

FIGURE 6.14: Interior design by Studio Ett Hem. In this slick Parisian apartment the designer cleverly segues from the living room to the staircase, adding display shelves, a picture gallery and an extra seat along the way.

DESIGNER — Darren Oldfield Architects

CLIENTS — Two professional families looking to maximise space in their existing homes

BRIEF — Two clients approached the architect with the same problem at around the same time – how to create a laundry room for a busy household without encroaching on the existing layout of the house more than necessary, and in keeping with the rest of the property. One of the families did not want to create a separate utility room as it meant losing their small family room, and the other was open to the idea of an extension to both kitchen and laundry, which could complement the existing house and make a more interesting rear elevation. They were also interested in creating a sustainable extension, including a green roof unseen from ground level.

LOCATION — Both houses are in South London. The projects were completed in 2018 and 2019.

CHALLENGE — The challenge for the first house was how to fit in the laundry, as well as finding space for various household paraphernalia. The architect suggested that a bank of cupboards would serve just as well as a laundry room, as they can be versatile while also looking very slick. They would also free up space that could be integrated into the rest of the house, which in this case left enough space for a small family room off the kitchen. The architect had to squeeze in not just the washing machine and tumble dryer, but also a sink, cleaning materials, toys, dog leads, vases and general household items that could be completely hidden.

FIGURES 6.15A AND 6.15B: Who would guess that a wall in this family room could contain so many household essentials?

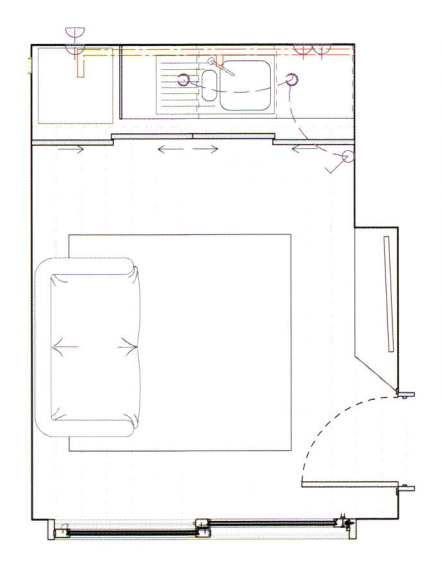

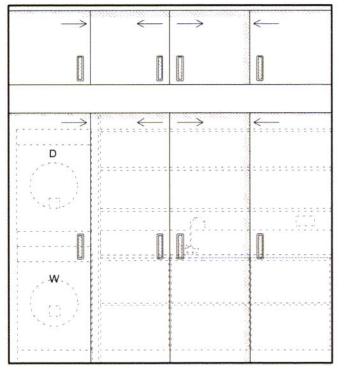

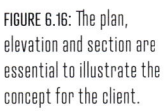

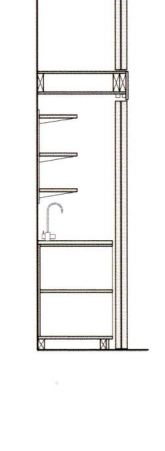

FIGURE 6.16: The plan, elevation and section are essential to illustrate the concept for the client.

FIGURE 6.17: The new elevation is visually arresting and reflects the existing rear elevation of the house.

FIGURE 6.18: The architect's elevation shows how the new pipework and joinery will enliven the rear facade.

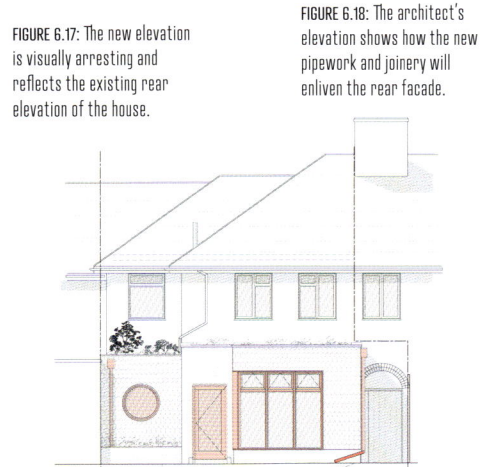

The second project was quite different. The clients were looking to extend the rear of their 1950s house to create a larger kitchen with a door to the garden and a useful utility room to the side. They wanted something that was visually interesting, while also being practical and in keeping with its surroundings. Both clients and architect were keen not to end up with an ubiquitous glass box design.

The architect suggested an extension in a combination of brick and hung tiles combined with funky red paint and a porthole window for the laundry. The stepped footprint of the extension takes into account the drainage and changes in level while creating a new rear elevation which is in keeping with the rear of the existing structure.

FIGURE 6.19: The pivoting porthole window creates an amusing focal point from both the inside and the outside of the building.

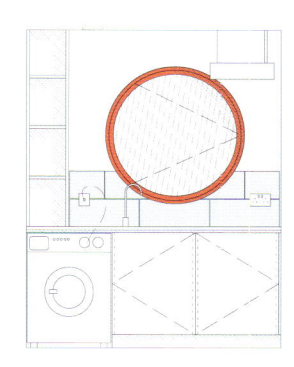

FIGURES 6.20A, 6.20B AND 6.20C: The architect's plan and elevation show the challenges in creating new drainage for the utility room with minimum disruption to the existing installation and the garden, while allowing for the changes between main house, extension and garden levels.

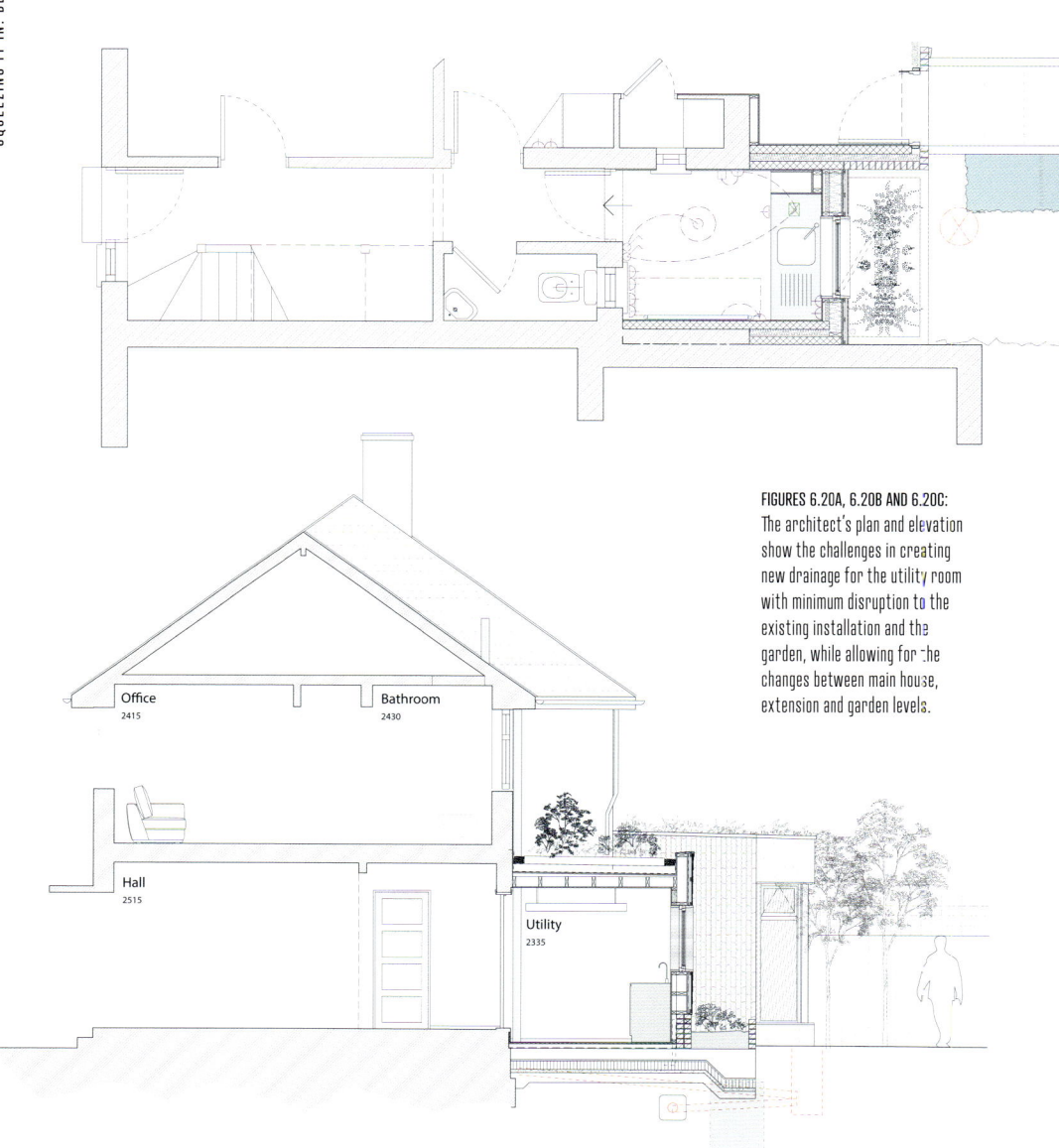

Office
2415

Bathroom
2430

Hall
2515

Utility
2335

Detailed architectural drawings were presented to the client as part of the process. These demonstrated the care the architects had taken to consider sustainable elements of the project. These included rainwater recirculation, so that a new aluminium hopper and downpipe gathered water from the roof and fed it into the planter below. These, along with all gutters and other pipework, were painted to match the new timber windows and part-glazed back door.

The existing window from the understairs WC, which looked into the utility room, was retained to give some natural light in an otherwise cupboard-like space. Air extraction for the utility room was by means of a mushroom vent in the new green roof above, negating the need for an unsightly vent in the new tile-hung outside wall.

The clients were able to use a ceiling-mounted laundry pulley, for which the joists above were reinforced to give a stable fixing. They also opted for plain cork tiles, which are a durable and easily maintained solution for the back premises of the house.

OUTCOME

Both clients wanted a way to have the laundry and other household chores kept out of sight of the rest of the house. For one family, the bank of cupboards enabled them to retain a family room, which might otherwise have been given over to a utility room. The large cupboards, with their plain tall doors and matching top cupboards, were a good-looking and practical solution to their problem. For the other family, the new utility room gave them the space they needed for a compact laundry and cloakroom. The witty porthole window was an interesting touch, which made an otherwise bland view from the hall into something much more inviting.

Both clients were delighted to have the space they needed created in such an imaginative way.

FIGURE 6.21: If a door is left open the view inside should be agreeable. The architect created a pleasing vista at the end of the narrow hallway with the witty porthole window and changes in finish between the hall and the laundry room.

CASE STUDY 6.2: MARY LESLIE INTERIOR DESIGN

DESIGNER	Mary Leslie
CLIENTS	A semi-retired couple downsizing to an art deco mansion flat in Central London
BRIEF	The clients required a kosher kitchen with a laundry/utility room attached and a small WC for children and the housekeeper. The laundry/utility room had to be multipurpose, and needed to include washer and dryer, sink, space for flower arranging, linen cupboards, an extra fridge/freezer, wine storage, a cupboard for cleaning materials, and an electrical cupboard for the consumer units, lighting controls and sound system. The flat was completely gutted, and the clients asked for a New England/Hamptons style throughout, with the exception of the back premises which were to be sleek, modern and easily maintained.
LOCATION	An art deco mansion block in Central London
CHALLENGE	Throughout the project the greatest challenge was locating the wet areas. The managing agents for the block and the tenants' committee had decreed after previous bad experiences that no tenant could extend the wet areas beyond the existing footprint. This meant the flat could have only two small bathrooms at the rear of the property, and neither the kitchen nor the utility room could be extended into the rest of the flat. When the block was built, people had a lesser expectation for the number and size of bathrooms, and the kitchen was much smaller than the clients might have wished. The space at the very rear of the property which the designer was allowed to use for the WC and laundry was limited to less than 4m².

FIGURE 6.22: Strict limitations on the wet areas allowed in this Central London flat meant all plumbing had to be squeezed into one corner of the room.

FIGURE 6.23: The stainless-steel work surface and plain cupboard fronts make the laundry room easy to maintain and a contemporary contrast to the rest of the flat.

The solution was to make a small WC beside the rear entrance, and to limit the wet space in the laundry to a stacked washer/dryer and a stainless-steel sink with a wall-mounted extendable tap above. For flower arranging the clients were given a fold-down table in front of the washing machine.

Once a suitable fridge/freezer had been found to fit the space by the kitchen door, the rest of the room was dedicated to cupboards. A low-level storage area with stainless-steel worktop in front of the window provided extra space for everyday tasks.

While the area may appear aesthetically simple it was challenging to fit everything in, and the client was very good-humoured about disposing of elements of her collection of linen and other household items as part of the downsizing exercise.

While the new joinery in the rest of the flat, including all cornices, skirting, architraves and panelling in the living room, bedrooms, hall and corridor, was designed to suit the Hamptons-style brief, the new laundry was quite different – with no panelling, practical and easily maintained surfaces, and no extraneous ornament. The floor was tiled with wide oak random plank to match the kitchen, and all the joinery remained white as part of the brief to keep the space efficient and clean.

A porthole in the swing door to the kitchen ensured that the small lobby at the back door would be safe, particularly when the clients were entertaining, and waiters were constantly passing back and forth.

The architectural draughtsman was very patient when the client, designer and the M&E consultants asked for small changes which improved the space without contravening the building constraints.

OUTCOME

The clients were delighted with the outcome, which meant that the household could run as smoothly as before, albeit in a space smaller than they had been accustomed to. They also appreciated the designer's attention to details such as the design of the WC and placement of food preparation, storage and refrigeration, ensuring they suited the clients' observant Jewish way of life.

FIGURE 6.24: The laundry room design is in complete contrast to the Hamptons-style kosher kitchen requested by the client.

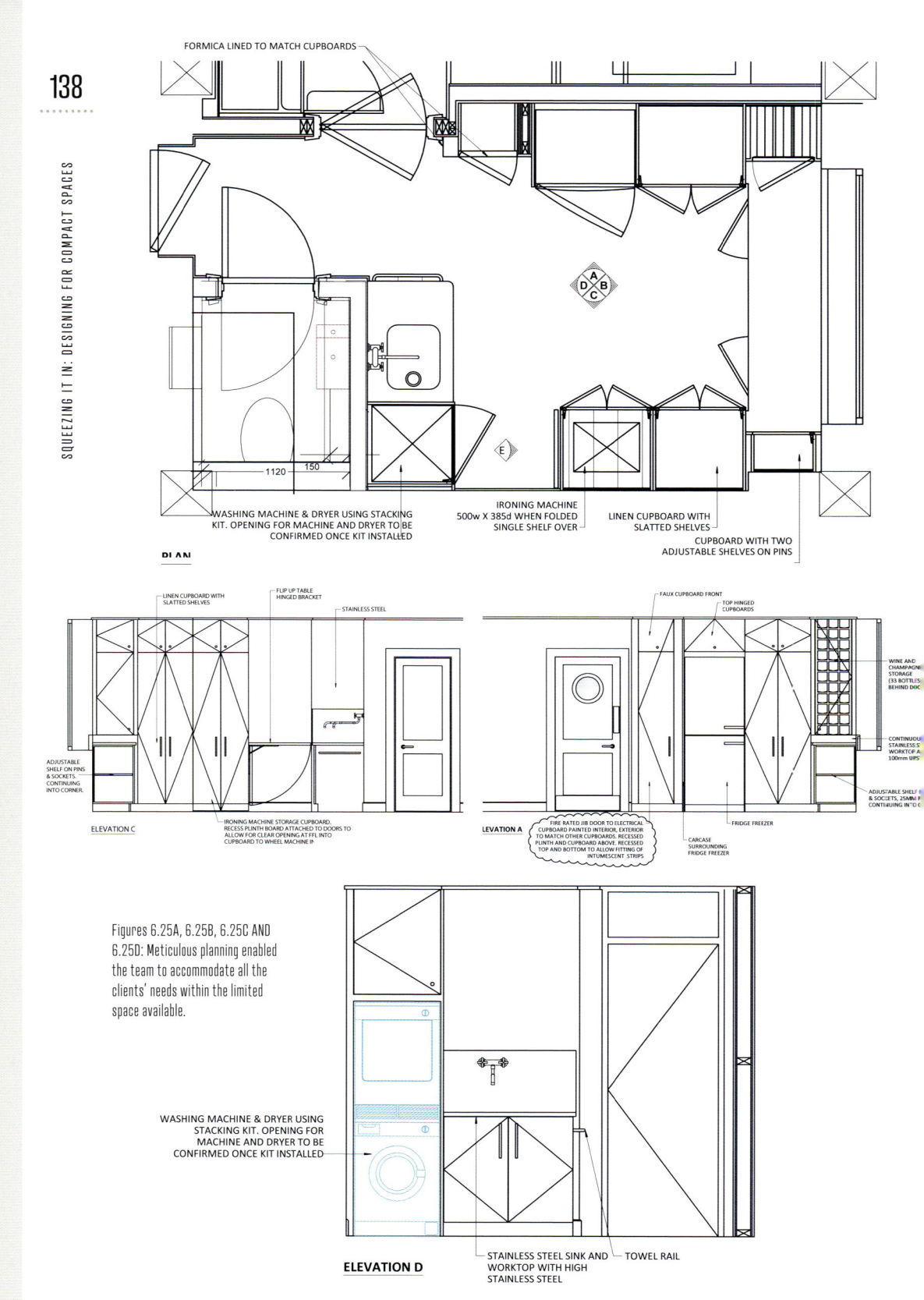

Figures 6.25A, 6.25B, 6.25C AND 6.25D: Meticulous planning enabled the team to accommodate all the clients' needs within the limited space available.

DESIGNER   Papa Architects designed the new basement extension. Cellar Maison designed the wine cellar and humidor.

CLIENTS   A North London family seeking to expand the space beneath their period property in Hampstead

BRIEF   The original brief was to create a new entertaining and leisure space beneath the existing house and garden. The client had a collection of fine wine and cigars he was keen to showcase; however, once the architects had included the main components of the new footprint there was little room for the cellar. It had to be visually exciting, contemporary, of the highest quality and with the correct temperature and humidity control for both wine and cigars.

Once the architects had located the ideal space for the wine feature, they commissioned a specialist wine cellar design company to design and build it.

LOCATION   A detached period property in Hampstead, North London

CHALLENGE   The whole basement area was an entirely new living space, within the curtilage of the existing period property. Fortunately, the original application to excavate the garden in 2007/08 was met with little resistance by the planners; a situation which might not be so easy post-2020, as local authorities become more reluctant to permit large-scale basement and garden excavations which may destabilise the ground and disrupt the neighbourhood. In optimising the space to accommodate the client's brief for a spacious wellness and living space, including an

6.26: A glamorous wine cellar fits into the stairwell as part of a major remodelling project in North London

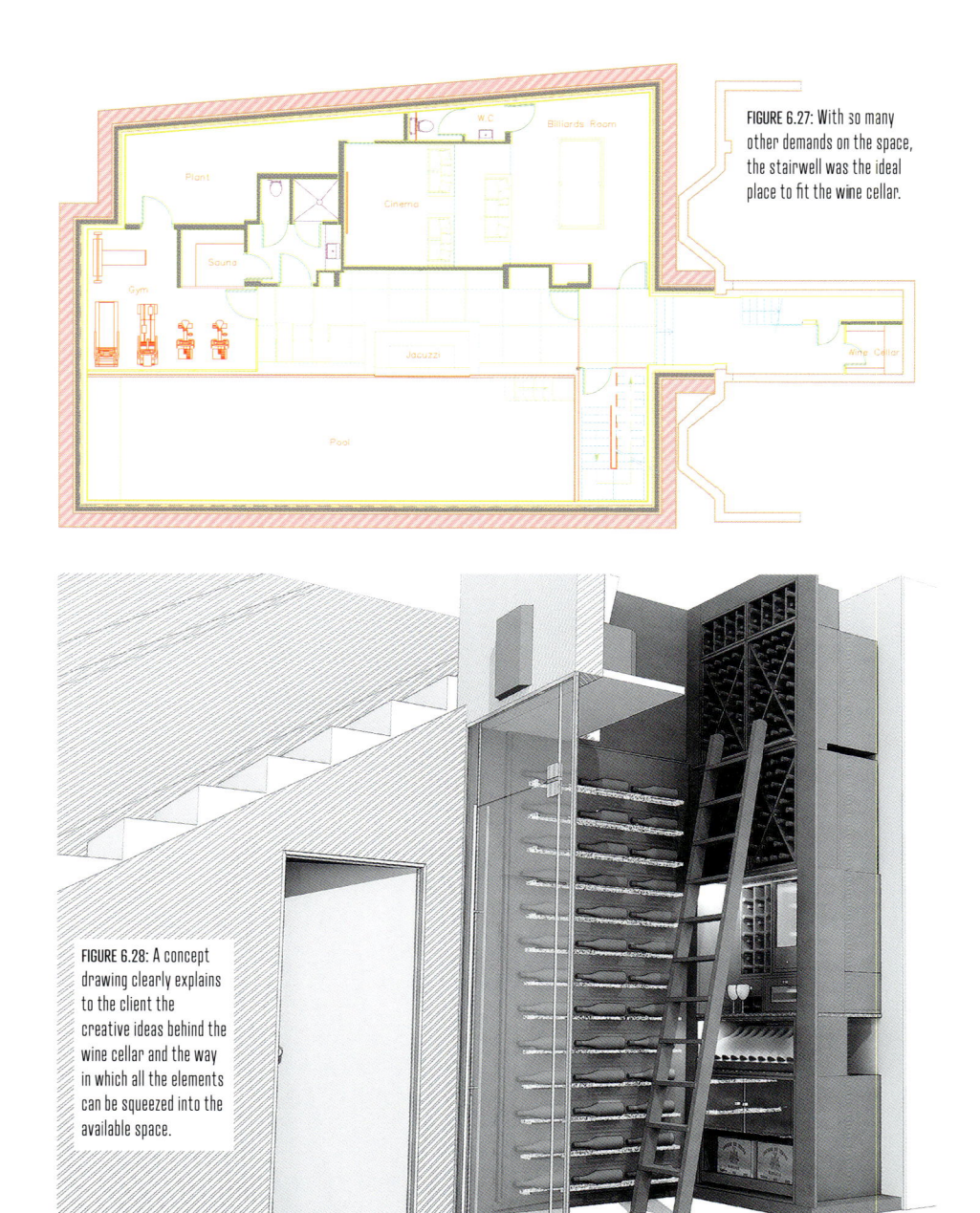

FIGURE 6.27: With so many other demands on the space, the stairwell was the ideal place to fit the wine cellar.

FIGURE 6.28: A concept drawing clearly explains to the client the creative ideas behind the wine cellar and the way in which all the elements can be squeezed into the available space.

indoor swimming pool, the architects were left with an awkward area below the staircase which measured only 1.2m wide by 1.8m deep. The staircase itself was positioned under the main staircase for the original house, which required detailed structural calculations and careful excavation of the space under the existing structure. However, the new stairwell was 3.7m high, which made an ideal space for a feature wine wall.

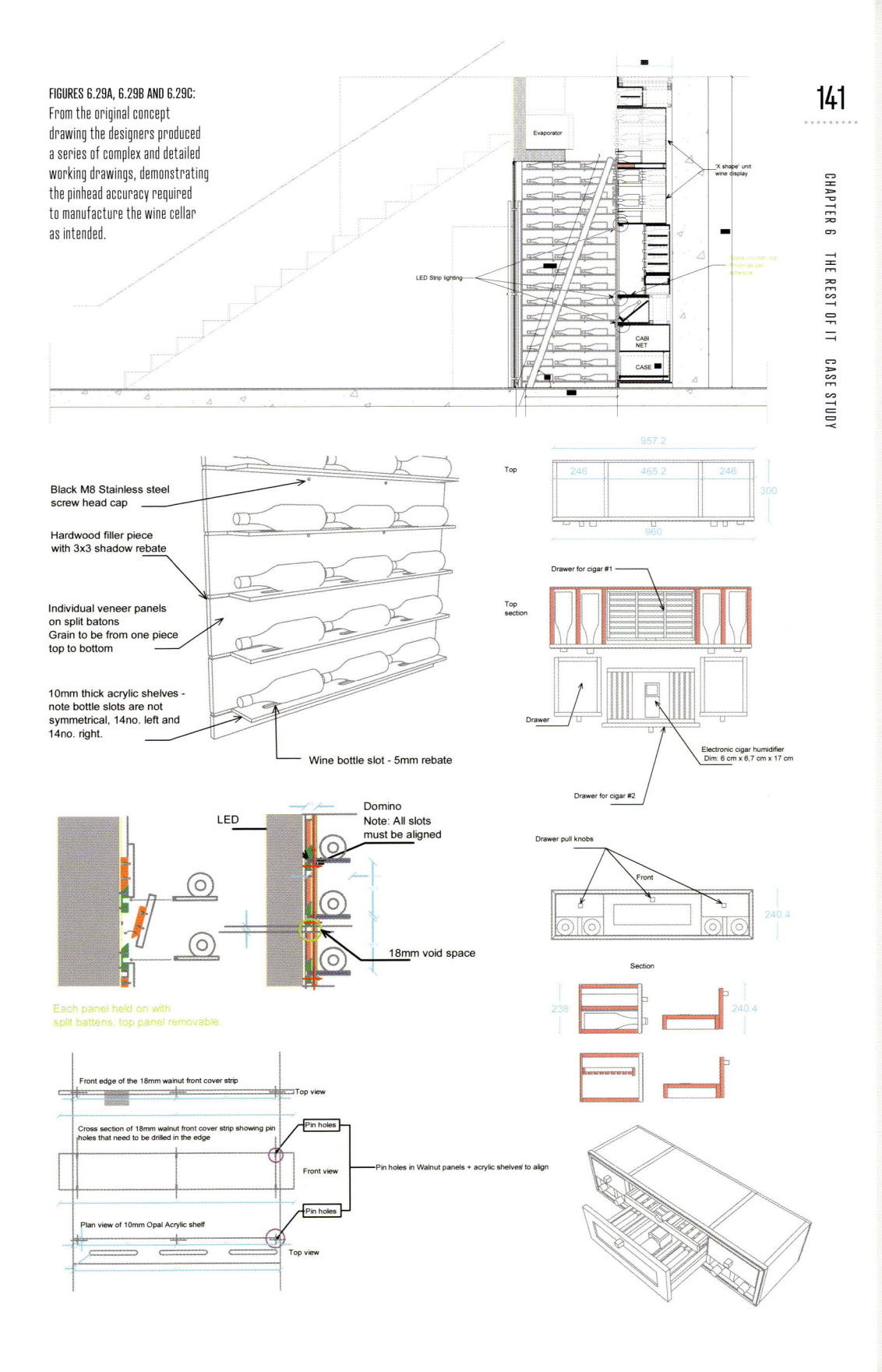

FIGURES 6.29A, 6.29B AND 6.29C:
From the original concept drawing the designers produced a series of complex and detailed working drawings, demonstrating the pinhead accuracy required to manufacture the wine cellar as intended.

Evaporator

'X shape' unit wine display

LED Strip lighting

CABI NET

CASE

Black M8 Stainless steel screw head cap

Hardwood filler piece with 3x3 shadow rebate

Individual veneer panels on split batons
Grain to be from one piece top to bottom

10mm thick acrylic shelves - note bottle slots are not symmetrical, 14no. left and 14no. right.

Wine bottle slot - 5mm rebate

Top

957.2

246   465.2   246

300

960

Top section

Drawer for cigar #1

Drawer

Electronic cigar humidifier
Dim: 6 cm x 6,7 cm x 17 cm

Drawer for cigar #2

Domino
Note: All slots must be aligned

LED

18mm void space

Each panel held on with split battens. top panel removable.

Drawer pull knobs

Front

240.4

Section

238   240.4

Front edge of the 18mm walnut front cover strip

Top view

Cross section of 18mm walnut front cover strip showing pin holes that need to be drilled in the edge

Pin holes

Front view

Pin holes in Walnut panels + acrylic shelves to align

Pin holes

Plan view of 10mm Opal Acrylic shelf

Top view

FIGURE 6.30: The fine detail of the acrylic shelves can be fully appreciated when seen from below.

FIGURE 6.31: The LED lighting catches the many different hues of wine, with bottles and labels forming an elegant surround to the central walnut display and the humidor.

The clients' brief was demanding, as they wanted to squeeze a great deal into such a small, but tall space – therefore, thoughtful and detailed design and engineering solutions were required to create a feature which worked both practically and aesthetically.

The client wanted to maximise bottle capacity for his fine wine collection, as well as include a small collection of cigars. The intention was to include a blend of classic and contemporary feature display shelving. The space was to be temperature and humidity controlled, and showcased behind lockable frameless glass. The wine to also had be accessible despite the 3.7m ceiling height.

The solution to storing and displaying sufficient wine with both contemporary and traditional storage areas was to combine narrow, cantilevered, edge-lit acrylic shelves running along the side walls, with a mixture of X-frame bins, racks and shelves for boxes. A feature section with stone shelf, drawers for accessories and the cigar humidor filled the centre of the back wall.

The designers opted for walnut as the most suitable wood for their purpose and used a combination of solid wood and veneer to give structural integrity to the design, while also enabling them to match cut veneers where specified.

The opal acrylic shelves running down the sides with their LED lighting strip in interchangeable colours had to be meticulously manufactured to ensure that they fitted the design, which had been carefully planned so that the electrical installation was hidden behind the veneer and acrylic sides to the wine cellar.

The single-panel 10mm toughened glass door was locked by means of a stainless-steel handle with integrated floor lock 2.2m high, and 35mm in diameter. A matching hydraulic bottom pivot patch fitting was the most discreet solution to maintain the frameless design of the door.

Given the height and small floor area, the designers introduced a library ladder, which could be unhooked and stored elsewhere. As the humidity and temperature requirements for the wine and the cigars are different, the designers implemented a compact through-wall cooling system with an additional humidifier within the cigar drawer.

OUTCOME

By using the height within the stairwell, the designers cleverly maximised the space to provide a striking, sophisticated and efficient wine wall which ideally suited the client, and provided a talking point as part of the new living space.

FIGURE 6.32: The view from above demonstrates how the wine cellar has become a desirable feature in the extension when seen from every angle.

7

THE ALL IN ONE

There will be times when the fortunate interior designer is involved in a new build or the complete remodelling of a property. That gives them the chance to include living, sleeping, cooking, working, wet areas and storage space as part of an overall concept rather than piecemeal. These are very exciting projects to be involved in, and while most new builds will also involve an architect, other projects may be within the interior designer's capabilities without the larger team. That gives the designer the chance to demonstrate their ability to manipulate space, work around services such as plumbing and electrics, accommodate the client's needs and provide furniture, furnishings and equipment in a truly creative way.

With the global increase in one-person households, there has been a corresponding increasing in the number of studio and one-bedroom homes. To make these interesting, the designer needs to avoid the formulaic and find unconventional solutions to using every inch of space available. Finding a space that might convert into such small apartments is exciting, but it is essential to consult an expert during the feasibility study. That might be an architect, surveyor or planning consultant who understands the local building and planning regulations. There will likely be restrictions on the minimum size of the apartments, and when considering low-cost housing or looking to convert existing spaces such as redundant offices into compact homes it is vital to take into account the physical and mental wellbeing of the target occupiers.

FIGURES 7.1A AND 7.1B: Mary Arnold-Forster Architects. Scotland, 2018. A series of sketches form part of a feasibility study for a development on a natural peninsula which once included a pier. The contemporary version would include 19 compact residential units and a cafe.

It only takes a single 'hook' for the designer's vision to take form. That might be a request from the client to use locally sourced finishes throughout. It might be the views outside, or a favourite artwork. If the project is speculative, the designer needs to find a look which will suit the site and appeal to as many prospective buyers as possible. Producing a quick sketch can be sufficient to capture the client's imagination.

The local authority may be concerned with the quality of the common parts of the development, and the developer with fitting as many units as possible into a small space, while a designer will ask – is there room to circulate around the furniture? Is there space to socialise? Why is it not possible to sit at the kitchen table and open the refrigerator door at the same time? Where will the ironing board go? In other words, how can we manipulate the space for the convenience of potential buyer or tenant? It may be that only small tweaks are needed to improve the space. A simple change, where cupboard space is limited, is to make a walk-in cupboard as a room divider. The living space footprint might be smaller, but having good storage makes for easier living, which is an enhancement to the space.

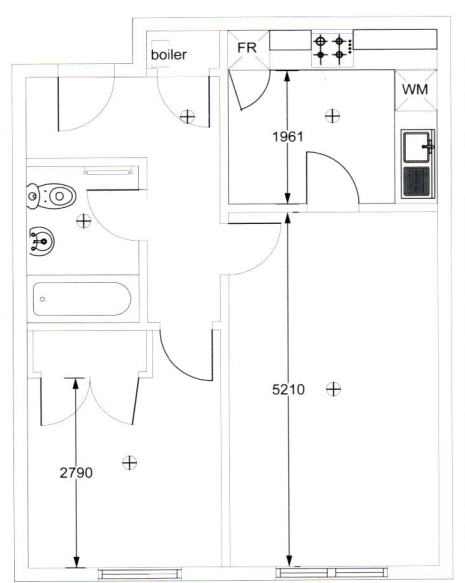

Affordable housing Kew. Existing layout

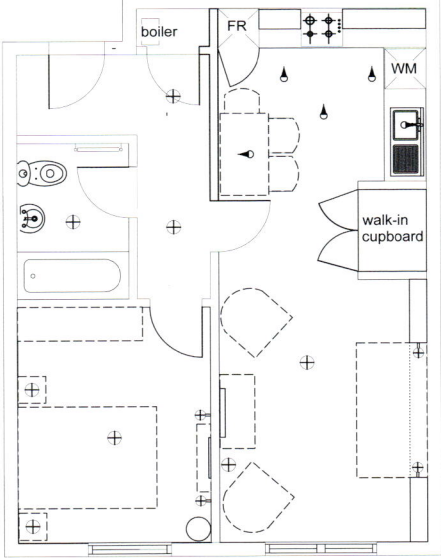

Affordable housing Kew. Proposed layout

FIGURES 7.2A, 7.2B AND 7.2C: Mary Leslie. London, 2008. Creating a walk-in cupboard between cooking and living spaces creates a practical and comfortable layout in this affordable housing unit in southwest London.

At the briefing stage the designer needs to have a very clear idea of the use for the property, so they are sure early on that the client's expectations are not unrealistic – and if they are, they need to be handled tactfully. The best way to overcome that is by offering alternatives. For example, moving internal walls, digging down, pushing out or up all help maximise the space. If extending is not an option, the designer needs to help the client compromise by working through the existing site and finding areas which can be multi-purpose, or a more appropriate use of the existing space.

Starting from scratch is an exciting proposition. Architects and designers who can develop a building from the foundations upwards or take something derelict and revive it have a fantastic opportunity to explore the possibilities of the space. They can exploit the volume to fit in all the functions of living, and whether their client wants a contemporary, transitional or traditional interior, they have the chance to create clever solutions within the limitations of the site. The project might be a 35m² studio flat or a 600m² house, but there will always be challenges to fitting everything into the space.

It is likely that an interior designer involved in a new build will be working with an architect. The architect will prefer to start from the outside and work inwards. However, it is the function of an interior designer to work from the inside out, ensuring that all of the day-to-day activities can be fitted into the available space. When the two disciplines meld successfully the results can be stunning. The designer will be able to point out, for example, that the items of furniture drawn on to the preliminary plans for ease of planning are not to scale, or that there is no room to squeeze between a chair and the door. How do you open the wardrobe doors and still fit a double bed into the room? These might seem basic errors, but they happen, and the interior expert as part of the team can solve them early. For both architect and interior designer, it is vital to consider the exterior when planning the interior, and taking advantage of light, orientation and views are good ways of making a property feel larger than it actually is.

A small all-in-one space might be a studio flat, a one-bedroom first-time buy, or a pied-à-terre. A larger property could be a holiday home or buy-to-let, or indeed a family home with a tight footprint and not much spare capacity. It might simply be that the designer is asked to incorporate cooking, eating and sitting into one multi-functional open-plan space which has to suit several age groups and activities at once, or find a way of moving everything around to turn an eighteenth-century cottage into something suitable for twenty-first-century living. When so much is being asked of these spaces, even if they appear at first to be large rooms, it is extraordinary how often experience shows that the design would be easier if they were six inches larger in each direction.

FIGURES 7.3A, 7.3B AND 7.3C: Mary Arnold-Forster Architects. Iona, Scotland, 2020. This new build home stands on the same footprint as its Doran bungalow predecessor. The compact, open-plan main room is designed to allow for comfortable family living while taking advantage of the stunning views across the sea.

Whichever type of project is being considered, the design team will be seeking to achieve optimum functionality combined with maximum impact in a restricted space. The limitations will be defined by the permissible footprint, local building regulations, and the client's requirements and budget. When refurbishing, they may be constrained by the age and size of the building, existing services, or permissions from the landlord in a leasehold property. These can make or break what seems a logical alteration for the designer and the clients, but if the district surveyor, landlord, tenants' association or management company raise objections to items such as plumbing alterations, hardwood floors or recessed light fittings, solutions can be expensive for the clients.

For example, if the property is a leasehold flat in a London mansion block, where the clients are required to lay acoustic materials below the proposed wood floor, the designer needs to understand the implications not just in terms of cost, but in potential loss of headroom too. Popping the skirtings, plinths and other joinery

FIGURE 7.4: Designed by Eva Byrne. Dublin. This living room in a Dublin new build may look large thanks to its high ceilings, but zoning is essential to make family living easier, and the dramatic artwork creates a clever visual break between sitting and dining areas, with sliding doors to cut off the kitchen beyond if necessary.

FIGURE 7.5: Interior design by René Dekker. London, 2015. A dramatic room divider separates sitting and dining areas in this London flat.

to accommodate the new acoustic sub-floor may not be practical, and will be an expensive exercise. Lawyers' and surveyors' fees soon mount up, and working with the building's management company needs to be handled professionally. Failure to comply might seem a small thing at the time but can prove difficult when the client comes to sell the property without the necessary licence.

If the brief is to design a living space where the clients can cook, eat and relax it has to be versatile, and zoning is the best way to achieve this. Can the cooking area be cut off from the rest by a sliding screen, or pocket or bi-fold doors? Are there alcoves or other spaces that can be exploited to give the suggestion of broken space? A large enough all-in-one living space can be zoned by the clever inclusion of sliding doors, or display units and bookshelves approached from both directions. Artwork can also be used to great effect to create a visual break between living spaces. Some amazing bespoke room dividers can be created using modern methods and materials. Taking a lead from North African and Middle Eastern designs, metal and wood can be used to create ornamental screens which are art forms in themselves. Clients interested in antiques may choose to hunt for old fretwork panels or doors, which can be recycled to give depth and character to a space.

In a small space where there is not enough room for a dining table, a breakfast bar will be ideal. Although clients love the idea, it is unlikely that there will be room for an island, which requires at least 900mm circulation space all around. A bar or peninsula approached from both sides can also serve as a barrier between cooking and eating, sitting or working.

If possible, the designer should try to create multiple seating areas to allow for eating, sitting and working. Even in a small space that can be done by mixing levels and creating visual barriers. Venetian or plantation shutters might be also used, along with sliding screens, fabric panels and blinds.

One of the difficulties with an all-in-one living space will be sound transmission. It is wise to avoid putting an extractor for the hob into the middle of the room, as it will interfere with anyone close by trying to listen to conversation, music or television. Throughout the space the use of carpet, rugs, soft furnishings and upholstery will help absorb the sound.

FIGURES 7.6A, 7.6B AND 7.6C: Interior design by Studio Ett Hem. Paris, 2020. Using natural barriers such as the exposed timber beams delineates the working, sitting, eating and cooking spaces in this top-floor Paris apartment.

The materials will be guided by the overall design concept. One client might request a dark, industrial look with strong architectural details made up of concrete, metal and glass. Another might prefer a clean, light palette, with plenty of pale wood, natural materials and white walls. As the designer will be aware, dark colours do not necessarily make a small space appear smaller, and the juxtaposition of dark and light with hard materials will make an arresting whole.

By contrast, an apartment built from pale wood can feel younger, and airier. Using bespoke joinery is a chance to create plenty of unexpected space to store or display possessions, and services such as cables and pipework can easily be hidden within the structure. Flat-panelled shelves and cupboards in various finishes of plywood are a clean and contemporary means of dividing a space where the client is looking for a simple, plain aesthetic that is good to look at and easy to maintain.

While pale-coloured woods which look light and youthful are also relatively inexpensive, alternative timbers such as walnut and zebrano, or bespoke finishes such as lacquer, make an apartment look highly sophisticated. That may be reflected in the deep pockets needed to pay for these finishes in large quantities.

The client will likely have priorities for the building, including environmental impact, sustainability and finishes, and for the rooms they need, or think they need. As mentioned earlier, the old-fashioned or habitual labels for rooms can helpfully be dropped in favour of their actual function. Thus the same open-plan space might serve as entrance hall, dining area, cooking space, living space and workspace. The upstairs landing might be the workspace; a corridor the library; the understairs becomes the laundry; and the bath is in the bedroom. Being playful with the spaces can produce surprising results.

When looking for ways of dropping the conventions and changing the layout to best advantage it may be possible to make the bath or shower part of the bedroom, leaving just a WC accessible from the hall for guests. Even in a one-bedroom flat an en-suite is regarded as preferable nowadays. If the apartment does not have space for two WCs, why not make the one accessible from the hall and keep the bath/shower private?

FIGURE 7.7: Interior design by René Dekker. London, 2016. With a WC tucked away elsewhere, the shower is cleverly squeezed into the bedroom of this top-floor Chelsea flat.

FIGURES 7.8A, 7.8B AND 7.8C: Darren Oldfield Architects and Beth Dadswell of Imperfect Interiors. London, 2019. The combination of mid-century and modern furniture together with plain colours and simple detailing ensure that this light-filled Notting Hill pied-à-terre flows effectively from front to back.

Every designer needs to be able to think in three dimensions to take advantage of space, but not every space has to be utilised: empty spaces also serve a purpose. Creating vistas within a property draws the eye and makes the space seem larger. There is also a curiosity about a view to another part of the home, or perhaps to the world beyond. A cleverly designed open-plan staircase creates a feeling of light and air, which makes a compact property feel larger than its footprint would suggest. Having the living areas above the sleeping space may make the best of a sloping site when services, wet spaces and storage need little or no natural light, but living, eating and cooking need as much light as possible.

As the layout begins to flow, the design team can use scale, proportion, detailing, colour and furnishings to make the whole feel balanced and harmonious. Every designer or architect understands the importance of scale and proportion. A compact space does not need to be dinky, but the detailing must be in proportion to the whole. Where a contemporary interior is distilled to its simplest form there may be no mouldings for the viewer to use as reference points, but the eye will soon discern whether an opening is too narrow or a ceiling too high.

When contemplating scale, the designer has to consider not only the relationship between objects, particularly when it comes to furniture, but also their scale in relation to the client. Small people do not like tall cupboards, and tall people do not appreciate low doorways.

Whilst considering the client's priorities, the general layout, proportion and scale the designer is seeking optimum functionality from the space. In order not to let that aim overwhelm the aesthetics of the whole, it is helpful to treat it like a three-dimensional geometry puzzle. A scale model is easy for the clients to understand, and to play with. They can see how the property sits in its surroundings, why the designs have developed as they have, and what alternatives there are within the building's envelope. Alternatively, a series of sketches or computer-generated images will help the clients appreciate the relationship between the spaces and the challenges involved in fitting the whole puzzle together.

A home needs to tell a story. The spaces may flow, but the furniture, furnishings and decoration need to be considered equally carefully. The decoration might be a backdrop for an art collection or hundreds of multi-coloured books, a home where the outside views matter most and the interiors are relatively understated, or one where a single, simple palette pulls the whole space into one. The designer needs to ensure that the architecture and the interior decoration are balanced so that neither detracts from the other. Too much symmetry and the interiors become too formal, duality confuses the eye, and a jumble of asymmetrical objects will only confuse. Styling subtle enough not to be obvious will make a harmonious interior with plenty of character. By repeating shapes, motifs and colours throughout the spaces the interiors become cohesive; however, the designer needs to ensure that they are not monotonous. While the colour palate or the furnishings may flow throughout, splashes of contrasting size, shape, colour and texture are needed to stimulate the eye.

FIGURES 7.9A AND 7.9B: Interior design by Studio Ett Hem. Paris, 2020. The tailored bespoke joinery, clever detailing and use of mirrors make this duplex seem larger than it really is. The change in decoration in the top-floor enfilade brightens the bedroom without detracting from the overall elegance of the interior.

The same lists of questions will apply for the all-in-one as they would if the designer were only involved in a smaller refurbishment project, but they must also keep asking themselves if the project has cohesion and harmony throughout.

Checklist — have you asked the client:

- Is there sufficient space for physical movement throughout the home?

- Even in a small space, are there vistas that catch the eye to give a sense of space?

- Has every available storage space been exploited? Could manipulating the space improve storage capacity?

- Has the best been made of the available natural light? Which spaces benefit most from any outside view?

- Has best use been made of layering artificial light throughout the space, using ambient, accent and task lighting?

- Will there be any problems with acoustics such as hard floors, extractor fans or plumbing to disturb the occupants or neighbours?

- Do the spaces flow naturally into one another, and are they in the best position (cooking beside eating, wet space beside sleeping space)?

- Is the furniture layout the most convenient for everyday living and entertaining?

- Are the proposed furnishings and finishes harmonious? When laying sample and mood boards beside one another, are the colours and textures balanced?

FIGURE 7.10: Jeffreys Interiors. Perthshire, Scotland, 2012. A high ceiling helps, but a tight footprint will always be a challenge in an open-plan living space. Stylish and cohesive furnishings pull together this former bothy living room.

CASE STUDY 7.1: STUDIO ETT HEM

DESIGNER	Pauline Lorenzi-Boisrond of Studio Ett Hem
CLIENT	A professional woman who was tired of staying in anonymous hotels on her frequent business visits to Paris
BRIEF	The brief was to transform a small student-style studio into a chic and cosy mini apartment under the eaves of a period building close to Saint-Germain-des-Prés. The only difference between a hotel and the flat would be the lack of room service.

In order to fulfil the initial brief, the former studio would need a discreet kitchen. The designer suggested creating an elegant entrance hall with three uses: kitchen, hall and dining corner. The double bedroom would exploit any space that could be used under the eaves, around the fireplace and in front of the new screen between kitchen and bedroom.

A neat shower room had to be fitted into the small space which housed the existing plumbing, and was entered through a gap in the load-bearing wall.

The designer needed to be very creative to squeeze everything into the existing 19m² studio, while instilling it with a feeling of sophistication, warmth and charm.

LOCATION	Paris, France
CHALLENGE	The challenge was to fit everything needed into a very small space.

The front door stood tight up against the structural wall, and could not be moved thanks to the long sloping ceiling; the latter also made circulation around a large part of the space difficult.

FIGURE 7.11: A view of the rooftops of Paris can be seen from every corner of this tiny apartment.

Figure 7.12: The original studio is divided to create cooking, living and sleeping spaces in miniature without feeling cramped, thanks to the combination of space planning, bespoke joinery, lighting, colour and texture.

FIGURE 7.13: The designer chose to create a barrier in the narrow space between the entrance door and the bedroom by inserting a glazed screen above the kitchen units.

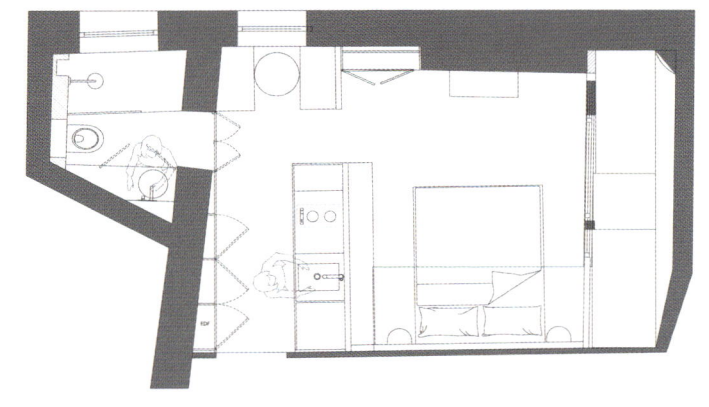

The designer proposed pushing everything against the walls, and created an attractive glazed screen above the kitchen units and bedroom storage. By very clearly defining the different spaces according to their function (sleeping, cooking, eating, toilet, reading) the space is made to look bigger.

The designer also managed to conserve traces of the age of this handsome early nineteenth-century building, such as the exposed beams, floor tiles and old fireplace.

The kitchen was perched on a platform so that it could be moved to the centre of the space, and to allow for essential services to run under the floor. A new *pointe de'Hongrie* (herringbone) parquet floor was laid through the cooking, eating and sleeping space, and subtly patinated to give the illusion of being original.

The angular, slanted wall in the hall was dressed by a series of doors with discreet mouldings, which conceal cupboards that become gradually shallower until the secret doors to the shower room, placed between two load-bearing walls.

The glazed screen between the bedroom and cooking area provides a barrier against sound, steam and smells, while still ensuring that plenty of light fills the centre of the space. The client could gaze out over the rooftops while preparing food, and the simple blinds do not detract from the view or take up valuable light.

The kitchen cupboards, walls and joinery merged one into another through the use of the same calm and sophisticated shade of blue, to envelop the space from floor to ceiling. The same theme ran through to

FIGURE 7.14: The bank of shallow cupboards with its secret doors to the shower room lead the eye towards the window and the comfortable dining nook. A *pointe de'Hongrie* floor also lengthens the room.

FIGURE 7.15: The bed tucked under the eaves is enhanced by the custom bedside tables with their splash of colour, and the carefully restored exposed beams.

FIGURE 7.16: Concealed behind panelled doors, the shower room appears larger than it is. Reflective tiles, a walk-in shower and plain floor all add to the calm feel of the space.

the fitted joinery in the bedroom, broken by the terracotta backs to the bedside table niches and the plain off-white walls. The restored exposed beams gave the space texture and character as well as paying homage to the age of the building, just as the client and designer intended.

Despite its awkward shape, the shower room contains a good-sized walk-in shower, WC and vanity unit with vessel basin and cupboard underneath. The space is easily maintained thanks to the minimal detailing and simple tiling throughout.

The client has options to sit at the dining table, or on a comfortable chair in the bedroom. Lighting is subtle throughout, and wall-mounted bedside lights either side of the bed hang neatly over the custom-built bedside tables, themselves recessed into the boxed-out dado-panelled wall behind the bed, which in turn conceals further services.

OUTCOME   The client now has a tiny retreat in the centre of Paris, full of character and delight, as well as being practical and low maintenance. The designer's clever appreciation for the space produced a cosy and charming pied-à-terre just as the client envisioned when she came across the student-style accommodation at the start of the journey.

FIGURE 7.17: Every part of the apartment is used to best advantage by carefully thought-out bespoke joinery or retaining original features such as the attic fireplace.

CASE STUDY 7.2: ATELIER FAVORI

FIGURE 7.18: When the sliding screens are in place this seems to be a small combined living room and kitchen.

DESIGNER   Kumiko Ishiguro of Atelier Favori

CLIENT   A young professional woman with a one-bedroom apartment which needed to be decorated and furnished

BRIEF   The brief was to create a comfortable home for a busy professional woman, including furnishings, furniture and equipment. As the apartment had already been modernised there was no need to disturb the layout. At only 45m² the space was limited but sufficient for everyday living.

In this typical layout for a one-bedroom apartment in Tokyo the small front room would be the tatami room, where most activities would be carried out on the floor, and which would contain tatami mats and plain wooden furniture to give the sense of calm and peace for which people strive as part of Japanese culture. However, in this instance the client asked for it to be turned into a study/bedroom so that family members could stay overnight in comfort.

The client also asked for a couple of comfortable armchairs and multi-purpose furniture so that she could entertain at a table in the small living room.

She wanted each room to have its own particular character, so that there would be visual interest when the screens between the various spaces were both open and closed.

LOCATION   A city centre apartment in Tokyo, Japan

Fortunately, there was no need to change the layout of the apartment as it had already been modernised; however, the designer was asked to propose and supply the furniture, fittings and equipment for the client's new home.

The sliding panels are veneered wood, and light enough to be easily manoeuvred. It was important that they were equally attractive from both sides. Symmetry was not as important as having the right number of doors for the space, and their size was more important than balance.

The apartment already had a good polished floor, so it was only necessary to provide a rug, which would create a visual anchor in the sitting area.

The living room and kitchen left very little room for a table at which to entertain, so the designer had a breakfast bar 50cm deep made, which tucked under the existing kitchen peninsula upstand and could be pulled out into the room to accommodate guests.

The client was fortunate that the apartment was large enough for the bedroom to have its own window. (If a room has no window it can only be referred to as a closet or store.) In this instance there was enough room for the space to have a comfortable bedroom and accommodate both the client's wardrobes and her piano. A neutral palette, freestanding furniture and luxurious fabrics combine to make a restful haven easily hidden by the siding screens.

FIGURE 7.19: With the screens pushed back, the whole apartment opens out to become a much larger space than it first seems.

FIGURE 7.20: Although the bedroom has its own window, it feels much airier when the screens are set back, showing the open-plan nature of the kitchen and living area.

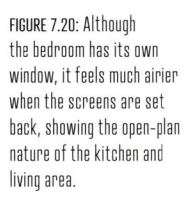

The designer had fun with the front room, and in place of the tatami mats and plain surroundings that would normally be found there she included a bright blue-and-white Toile de Jouy wallpaper, desk, guest closet and comfortable sofa bed. The views from both windows were framed by plain Venetian blinds with no curtains, for simplicity. A witty touch was the set of gilt frames with glass inserts but no images which hang over the sofa.

OUTCOME

One of the advantages of an apartment that uses sliding screens in place of walls and doors is the ability to make the spaces public or private according to need. If guests are present, the sliding screens can be closed for privacy. When the whole flat is in use the screens can be left open to give light and air throughout. This also allows different vistas to open up, which is an important way of making a space seem larger, however compact it may be.

By using simple, cheerful and comfortable furniture and furnishings combined with amusing accessories, the designer created an ideal home for a young woman starting out on her professional life in a busy city.

FIGURE 7.21: The original tatami room is transformed into a study/bedroom by the cheerful wallpaper and comfortable sofa bed.

FIGURE 7.22: Vistas are vital even in small apartments, and the view from sofa to television screen gives the illusion of a larger space than it actually is.

CASE STUDY 7.3: THORP

DESIGNER   Philippa Thorp of THORP

CLIENT   The clients were a semi-retired English couple with whom the designer had worked previously, so they had already built up a relationship of trust. The house would be used during the week while the teenage children were at school and the parents busy with their own lives.

BRIEF   The clients found a small terraced cottage in need of renovation. They were very open-minded about reaching a solution, but their initial brief was exacting. They asked for three bedrooms and three bathrooms, with a living room open to the kitchen and space for six to sit comfortably at a table. They also wanted to have a small entrance lobby to avoid stepping straight from the street into the sitting area.

The house needed to be as orderly, functional and serene as a hotel suite, with neutral colours such as off-white, cream and pale blue – in contrast to their house in the country, which was very colourful.

LOCATION   The property was a pink Chelsea cottage which needed to be completely renovated to suit the brief. All the houses in the street were different colours, some renovated and some not.

FIGURE 7.23: A small cottage can be as complex as a large house to turn into something very special.

The project was a designer's dream. Her first reaction on seeing the house was that to fulfil the brief it would be necessary to move the staircase. It would have to be reconfigured to accommodate the services for the three bathrooms. Once it had been shifted to the other side of the house the rest fell into place, and the designer's team were able rearrange the ground floor and strike a new straight line to the side of the enlarged living room, which enabled them to drop the services down behind the panelling between sitting and dining areas.

The planners were very open to the idea of moving the staircase, and accommodating in agreeing to the plan, as some houses in the street already had extra glazing at the back. Although the staircase would be glazed almost top to bottom, the southwest elevation was not overlooked, so it would always give suitable privacy for the family. The glazing for the new staircase would run to the top of the kitchen extension, which was given extra roof lights for natural daylight. The roof lights formed part of the roof terrace accessed from the new master bathroom.

The designer's view, beyond the functional, was that a house needs a good staircase to succeed. The drawings showed that it would be tight but workable. It needed to have gentle going, which the original did not. The new staircase was a steel structure clad in timber, which allowed the designer to use the volume like a corkscrew.

FIGURES 7.24A AND 7.24B:
By moving the staircase from the position shown in the layout in Figure 7.24a to the proposed layout in Figure 7.24b, the jigsaw starts to fall into place.

The house had no basement, and the ground floor was dropped by 150mm to improve the proportion of the space. A laundry cupboard was carved out of the space under the stairs to include the smallest possible washer and dryer, well out of sight.

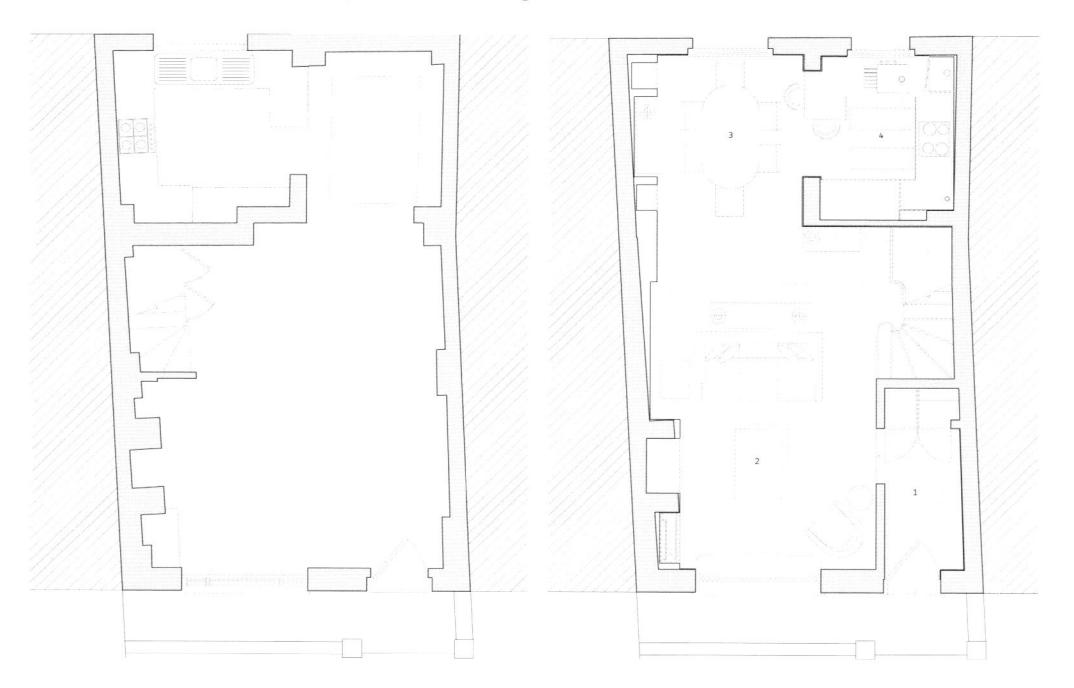

The open-plan living room and kitchen were reconfigured to give a comfortable sitting area at the front of the cottage with space for a dining room beside the highly functional kitchen. The whole space is opened up by the new staircase and the wide random plank floor with a simple cream rug to delineate the seating area at the front.

To keep to the brief, the designer specified a contemporary kitchen with white Parapan® cupboard and drawer fronts. The small peninsular allowed the family to have quick meals without using the dining table. Services including the boiler were hidden in the space between the new kitchen and the staircase.

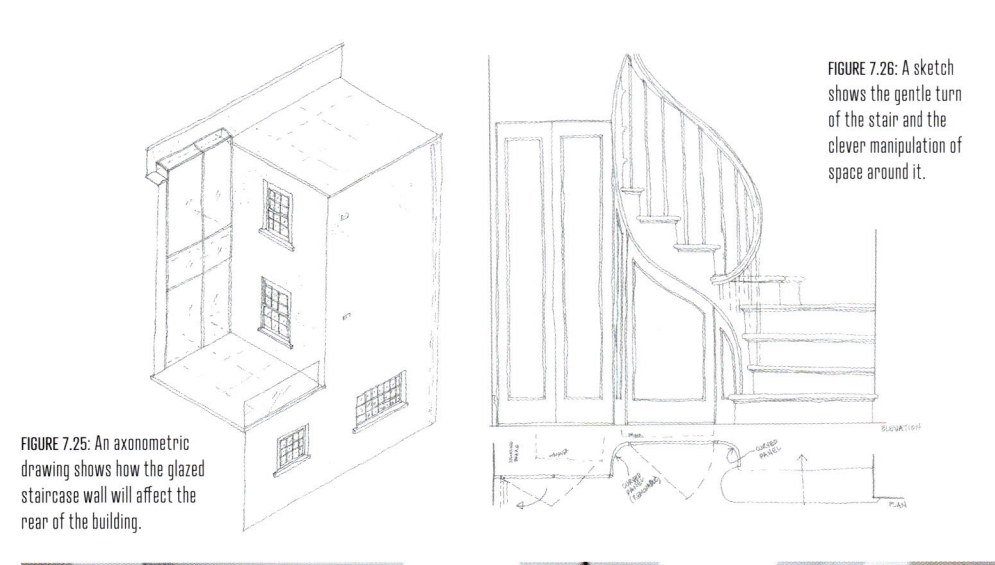

FIGURE 7.26: A sketch shows the gentle turn of the stair and the clever manipulation of space around it.

FIGURE 7.25: An axonometric drawing shows how the glazed staircase wall will affect the rear of the building.

FIGURE 7.27: The high-gloss, flat unit fronts and exploitation of every available space ensure that the clients' request for everything possible to be out of sight is fulfilled.

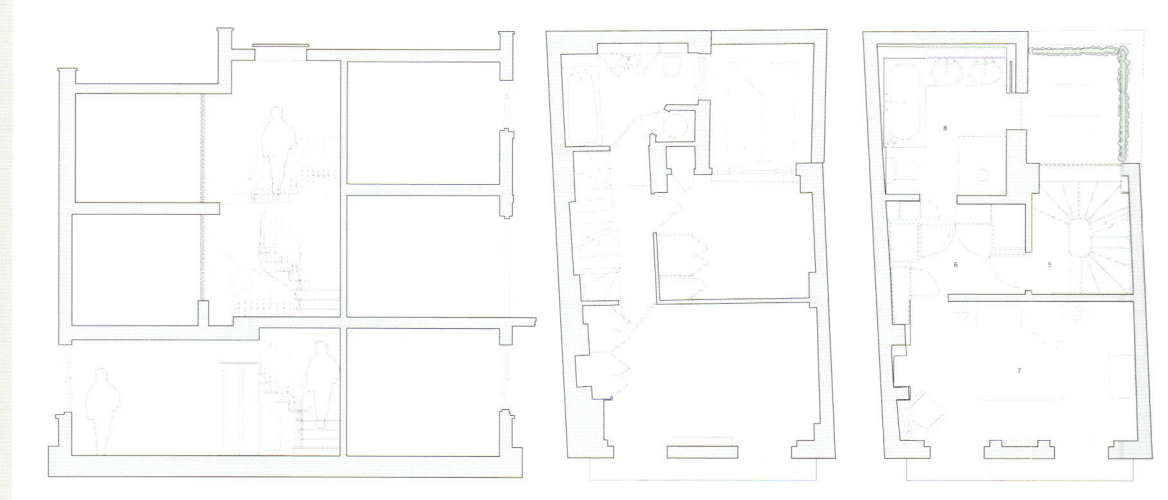

FIGURES 7.28A, 7.28B AND 7.28C: The section and first floor before and after drawings demonstrate the need to consider changes in floor level on the upper floors when reconfiguring the rooms.

FIGURE 7.29: The bathroom appears more spacious than it is by clever use of bespoke cabinets, panelled mirrors and discreet toplighting

For the first floor the designer created a compete master suite including a comfortable bedroom, ample wardrobe space and a luxurious and spacious bathroom, which included separate bath, shower and two basins. The designer used the same trick of squaring off the fire surround to improve the look. She also compensated for the change in level between front and back of the house by dropping down between the dressing area and bathroom on the bathroom side but keeping the door on the same plane as the wardrobes.

The master bathroom gained an illusion of space by creative use of mirrors, and a predominantly cream colour palette. Plenty of storage space was included by setting a pair of vessel basins over a bank of cupboards between the bath and the French window out on to the roof terrace. Both the sitting room and the master bedroom had gas fires, which would be both glamorous and convenient.

Careful attention was also paid to the top floor, where the designer had to squeeze two bedrooms and shower rooms into the available space. The children's bedrooms needed wardrobe space and somewhere for the children to study during the week.

The designer specified fabric walling for the bedrooms, which would both soften the sound and give the rooms texture. By using a restrained palette of creams, off-white and soft tones throughout she created an illusion of space which belies the tiny footprint of the little Chelsea cottage.

OUTCOME

The clients were happy to have a house which fulfilled the brief, and the designer was satisfied that the outcome was practical to use and pleasing to behold.

FIGURES 7.30A AND 7.30B: The top floor bedrooms have sufficient light and space for the teenagers, as well as giving them the privacy of their own shower rooms.

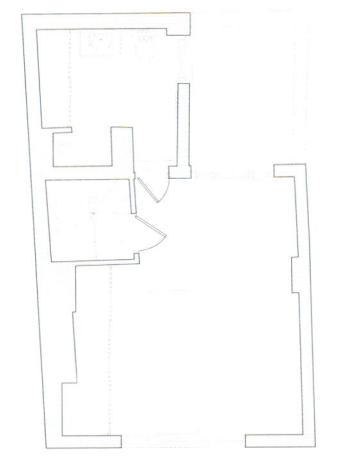 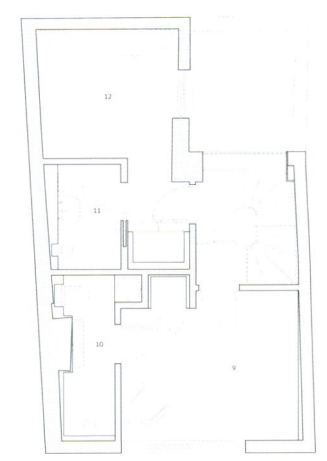

FIGURE 7.31: A view down the staircase reveals the amount of detail which is needed to squeeze a beautifully crafted object into a very compact space.

INDEX

IMAGE CREDITS

Figure 0.0: © Alma Ltd

Figure 0.1 & 0.5: Designed by Mary Arnold-Forster, MAFA, © Andrew Lee Photographer

Figure 0.2: © John Lees

Figure 0.3a-b: Designed by Harriet Hughes, © ZAC and ZAC

Figure 0.4: © Mary Leslie Interior Design

Figure 0.6: © Mellis Haward, Archio

Figure 0.7: Architecture by Darren Oldfield Architects, Interior Design by Beth Dadswell, Imperfect Interiors, © Chris Snook Photography

Figure 1.0: Designed by the Manser Practice, © Alexander James Photography

Figure 1.1a-b: Designed by Harriet Forde, © ZAC and ZAC

Figure 1.2a-c & 1.6a-b: © Mary Leslie Interior Design

Figure 1.3a-c: Designed by MW Architects for Solid Space, © French+Tye

Figure 1.4 & 1.8: © René Dekker

Figure 1.5: © Eva Byrne

Figure 1.7: Designed by Mary Leslie Interior Design, © Neale Smith Photography

Figure 1.9: Styled by Flora Bathurst, Designed by Spencer & Wedekind, © Felix Speller Photography

Figure 1.10: Designed by Mary Leslie Interior Design, © Mary Leslie Interior Design

Figure 1.11: Styled by @thegirlwiththegreensofa, © Maria Helena Ltd.

Figure 1.12, 1.14, 1.16 & 1.17: Designed by Archio, © French+Tye

Figure 1.13a-b & 1.15: Designed by Archio, © Archio

Figure 1.18, 1.21, 1.22 & 1.23: Styled by Hannah Simmons, Designed by Spencer & Wedekind, © Sarah Hogan Photography

Figure 1.19 & 1.20: © Spencer & Wedekind

Figure 2.0: Designed by MW Architects, © French+Tye

Figure 2.1a-c: Designed by Spencer & Wedekind, © Felix Speller Photography

Figure 2.2: © Maria Helena Ltd.

Figure 2.3a-c: Designed by Mary Leslie Interior Design, © Mary Leslie Interior Design

Figure 2.4a Designed by Mary Arnold-Forster, © Mary Arnold-Forster, MAFA

Figure 2.4b & 2.7: Designed by Mary Arnold-Forster, © David Barbour Photography

Figure 2.5: © Geoffrey Jackson, Langley Furniture Works

Figure 2.6a-c & 2.8: © Eva Byrne

Figure 2.9: © René Dekker

Figure 2.10: Designed by Jo Duerden of Design by Jo Bee Ltd., © Heidi Marfitt Photography

Figure 2.11a-b: © Armstrong Keyworth

Figure 2.12: Designed by Benjamin Tindall Architects for Blue Cabin by the Sea, © Benjamin Tindall Architects

Figure 2.13, 2.16 & 2.17: © Keith Hunter Photography

Figure 2.14 & 2.15: Designed by Benjamin Tindall Architects, © Benjamin Tindall Architects

Figure 2.18, 2.19, 2.20a-c, 2.21 & 2.22: Designed by Mary Leslie Interior Design, © Mary Leslie Interior Design

Figure 2.23 & 2.28: Designed by Jeffreys Interiors and Peden & Pringle, © ZAC and ZAC

Figure 2.24: © ZAC and ZAC

Figure 2.25, 2.26 & 2.27: © Peden & Pringle

Figure 3.0: Designed by Mary Arnold-Forster, MAFA, © David Barbour Photography

Figure 3.1, 3.11 & 3.13: Styled by Flora Bathurst, Designed by Spencer & Wedekind, © Felix Speller Photography

Figure 3.2a-b: Designed by Spencer & Wedekind, © Felix Speller Photography

Figure 3.3: Architecture by Darren Oldfield Architects, Designed by Beth Dadswell, Imperfect Interiors, © Chris Snook Photography

Figure 3.4: © Eva Byrne

Figure 3.5: Designed by 2LG Studio, © Megan Taylor

Figure 3.6 & 3.7: Designed by HÁM Interiors, © Alexander James Photography

Figure 3.8, 3.9, 3.10, 3.15, 3.16, 3.17, 3.18 & 3.19: Designed by Mary Leslie Interior Design, © Mary Leslie Interior Design

Figure 3.12: Designed by Benjamin Tindall Architects for Blue Cabin by the Sea, © Benjamin Tindall Architects

Figure 3.14: Designed by Chris Dyson, © Alexander James Photography

Figure 3.20, 3.22a, 3.22c & 3.24: Styled by Hannah Simmons, Designed by Spencer & Wedekind, © Sarah Hogan Photography

Figure 3.21, 3.22b & 3.23a-b: © Spencer & Wedekind

Figure 4.0: © René Dekker

Figure 4.1, 4.3, 4.14, 4.15, 4.16 & 4.17: Designed by Plankbridge Ltd., © Plankbridge Ltd.

Figure 4.2, 4.5 & 4.8: Designed by Mary Leslie Interior Design, © Mary Leslie Interior Design

Figure 4.4a & d, 4.7 & 4.9: Designed by MW Architects, © French+Tye

Figure 4.4b & c Designed by Matthew Wood, © MW Architects

Figure 4.6: © Mary Leslie Interior Design

Figure 4.10, 4.11 & 4.12: Designed by Dean Keyworth, © Clarion Events

Figure 4.13: Designed by Dean Keyworth, © Clarion Events. Leather Dice chair with arms designed by David Linley, © Clarion Events.

Figure 5.0: Styled by Flora Bathurst, Designed by Spencer & Wedekind, © Felix Speller Photography

Figure 5.1 & 5.13d: Designed by 2LG Studio, © Megan Taylor

Figure 5.2, 5.8, & 5.13c: Designed by Mary Leslie Interior Design, © Mary Leslie Interior Design

Figure 5.3a-b: Designed by Field Day Studio, © Astrid Templier Photography

Figure 5.4a: Designed by Izat Arundell, © ZAC and ZAC

Figure 5.4b: Designed by Spencer & Wedekind , © Astrid Templier Photography

Figure 5.5a: Designed by Studio Duggan, © Alexander James Photography

Figure 5.5b: Designed by Valentin Tatanov, © Tadelaktlondon.co.uk

Figure 5.6: © Mairi Helena Ltd.

Figure 5.7 a-b: Designed by Guy Goodfellow, © Guy Goodfellow

Figure 5.7c: Designed by Guy Goodfellow, drawings by Richard Lansley Designs, © Guy Goodfellow

Figure 5.9a: Designed by Studio Ett Hem, © BCDF

Figure 5.10 & 5.11: Designed by Mary Leslie and David Morris of Lambert Smith Hampton, © Mary Leslie Interior Design

Figure 5.12: Designed by Life Design London, © ZAC and ZAC

Figure 5.13a: Designed by Darren Oldfield Architects, © Guy Lockwood Photography

Figure 5.13b: Designed by Benjamin Tindall Architects for Blue Cabin by the Sea, © Benjamin Tindall Architects

Figure 5.14: Designed by Jeffreys Interiors, © ZAC and ZAC

Figure 5.15, 5.19 & 5.20: Architecture by Darren Oldfield Architects, Interior Design by Beth Dadswell, © Chris Snook Photography

Figure 5.16, 5.17a-b & 5.18: © Darren Oldfield Architects

Figure 5.21 & 5.22: Designed by Kumiko Ishiguro, © Mr Nobutake Sawasaki

Figure 5.23, 5.24, 5.25 & 5.26: © Kumiko Ishiguro, Atelier FAVORI

Figure 5.27, 5.28, 5.29 & 5.30: © MW Architects

Figure 5.31 & 5.32: Designed by MW Architects, © French+Tye

Figure 6.0: Designed by Jeffrey Interiors, © ZAC and ZAC

Figure 6.1a-b, 6.5a-b, 6.7a, 6.15a-b, 6.17, 6.19 & 6.21: Designed by Darren Oldfield Architects, © Guy Lockwood Photography

Figure 6.2, 6.3 & 6.4: © Eva Byrne

Figure 6.5c, 6.7b, 6.16, 6.18 & 6.20a-c: © Darren Oldfield Architects

Figure 6.6: © Armstrong Keyworth

Figure 6.8: © Cellar Maison Ltd.

Figure 6.9: © @homefunkyhome

Figure 6.10: Designed by Mary Arnold-Forster, MAFA, © David Barbour Photography

Figure 6.11: © René Dekker

Figure 6.12: Designed by 2LG Studio, © Megan Taylor

Figure 6.13: © Jamie Adams, @wheelspin_chesham

Figure 6.14: Designed by Studio Ett Hem, © BCDF

Figure 6.22, 6.23, 6.24 & 6.25 a-d: Designed by Mary Leslie Interior Design, © Mary Leslie Interior Design

Figure 6.26, 6.28, 6.29a-c, 6.30, 6.31 & 6.32: Designed by Cellar Maison, © Cellar Maison Ltd

Figure 6.27: Architecture by Papa Architects, © Papa Architects Ltd

Figure 7.0: Designed by Izat Arundell, © ZAC and ZAC

Figure 7.1a-b: Designed by Mary Arnold-Forster, MAFA, © David Barbour Photography

Figure 7.2a-c & 7.3a-c: Designed by Mary Leslie, © Mary Leslie Interior Design

Figure 7.4: © Eva Byrne

Figure 7.5 & 7.7: © René Dekker

Figure 7.6a-c & 7.9a-b: Designed by Studio Ett Hem, © BCDF

Figure 7.8a-c: Architecture by Darren Oldfield Architects, Interior Design by Beth Dadswell, Imperfect Interiors, © Chris Snook Photography

Figure 7.10: Interior Design by Jeffreys Interiors, © ZAC and ZAC

Figure 7.11, 7.13, 7.14, 7.15, 7.16 & 7.17: Interior Design by Studio Ett Hem, © BCDF Studio

Figure 7.12: © Studio Ett Hem

Figure 7.18, 7.19, 7.20, 7.21 & 2.22: Interior design by Atelier FAVORI, © Way Co. Ltd.

Figure 7.23 & 7.27: Interior Design by THORP, © James Merrell Photographer

Figure 7.24a-b, 7.25, 2.26, 7.28a-c & 7.30a-b: Architecture and Interior design by THORP, © THORP

Figure 7.29 & 7.31: Interior Design by THORP, © Niall Clutton Photography